Assorted Candies for the Theatre

WITHDRAWN

Assorted Candies for the Theatre

Michel Tremblay

translated by
Linda Gaboriau

Talonbooks

Talonbooks
P.O. Box 2076, Vancouver, British Columbia, Canada V6B 3S3
www.talonbooks.com

Typeset in New Baskerville and printed and bound in Canada.
Printed on 100% post-consumer recycled paper.

First Printing: 2007

The publisher gratefully acknowledges the financial support of the Canada
Council for the Arts; the Government of Canada through the Book Publishing
Industry Development Program; and the Province of British Columbia through
the British Columbia Arts Council and the Book Publishing Tax Credit for our
publishing activities.

Bonbons assortis au théâtre was first published in French by Leméac Éditeur in 2006.

Library and Archives Canada Cataloguing in Publication
Tremblay, Michel, 1942–
[Bonbons assortis au théâtre. English]
    Assorted candies for the theatre / Michel Tremblay ; translated by
Linda Gaboriau.

Translation of: Bonbons assortis au théâtre.
A play.
ISBN 978-0-88922-572-5

    I. Gaboriau, Linda II. Title. III. Title: Bonbons assortis au théâtre. Anglais.

PS8539.R47Z46413 2007   C842'.54   C2007-901060-1

This play, inspired by the collection of stories *Bonbons assortis*, was first produced in French on March 28, 2006 at Théâtre du Rideau Vert, Montreal, in a production directed by René Richard Cyr, with the following cast:

LE NARRATEUR:	Gilles Renaud
NANA:	Rita Lafontaine
ALBERTINE:	Adèle Reinhardt
VICTOIRE:	Pierrette Robitaille
GABRIEL:	Germain Houde
JOSAPHAT:	Pierre Collin
LISE ALLARD:	Sandrine Bisson
Assistant Director:	Isabelle Brodeur
Set Design:	Richard Lacroix
Props:	Éliane Fayad
Costumes:	Marie-Pierre Fleury
Lighting:	Michel Beaulieu
Music:	Alain Dauphinais

*For my cousin, Jeannine Laurin
who would have so many tales to tell
about this same period ...
with all my affection.*

Characters

THE NARRATOR
NANA, in her late forties
ALBERTINE, in her mid-forties
VICTOIRE, in her sixties
LISE ALLARD, in her twenties
GABRIEL, in his late forties
JOSAPHAT, in his late sixties

Act One

THE NARRATOR will participate in the action, saying little Michel's lines in his adult's voice, as if he were there with the others.

During the opening monologue, THE NARRATOR is comfortably ensconced in his favourite armchair where he does his best daydreaming.

THE NARRATOR

Memory is a mirror that chooses what it wants to reflect. Memory is a mirror that distorts. And cheats. And lies. Memory can embellish things or make them ugly, it interprets as it sees fit and draws its own conclusions. And all too often our memory leads us down paths that our conscience would advise us to avoid, but those paths seem so promising and irresistible. Memory revives events that never happened and obliterates important facts, it emphasizes the most absurd trivia and chooses to forget essential details. In short, our memory fabricates a distorted image of the past, then imposes it as gospel truth when it's really just a sketchy interpretation—but always more interesting, livelier and more vivid than reality. Memory is the mother of invention. And the big sister of imagination. Everything you'll see in the following scenes really happened when I was a child ... at least, the facts are true, the bare bones, the anecdote, the essence of the story—it could all be corroborated and told by someone else who was there at the time, but my memory of these events, my interpretation of these events, and most of all, my way of relating them are dictated by my personal mirror which, you will soon see, had a field day. The story

9

someone else might tell would undoubtedly be very different. At least in style. In one of my other plays, the same mother you'll meet here tonight told her son that things are never interesting enough to be described as is. I think that is my memory's motto. To my great delight when I'm writing, because there's nothing I enjoy more in life than resuscitating these characters from my childhood, painting their portraits and letting them speak for themselves ... and to your delight, too, I suppose, since you chose to pay good money to come and watch what will happen on this stage over the next hour or two. Of course, I run the risk of disappointing you. But that's a risk I'll have to take. I did what I could with what I had. Recreating everything with the help of the mother of invention and the big sister of imagination.

The lights go up on the dining room of a typical 1940s Montreal flat. When the action takes place elsewhere, the lights will go down on this room. NANA, ALBERTINE and VICTOIRE are sitting around the dining table, counting money.

THE NARRATOR

Don't try to find me, I'm hiding under the table, as usual, listening to everything being said above me. It's hot in my hiding place, and everything smells of soap and cheap per- fume, of varnished wood and the old braided rug, and sometimes I have to get out of the way because feet wearing scratchy wool or fuzzy angora slippers are constantly shifting all around me. When the women open their legs, I catch a glimpse of white underpants, loose in my mother's case, elasticized above the knee for my grandmother, and thread- bare from too much bleach in the case of my aunt Albertine. Sometimes those legs shift and I receive the occasional kick—an accident when it's my mother, but when it's one of the other two women, I know they're simply checking to see if I'm still there. If I were not there, things would be said differently, less cautiously, more clearly. But I'm almost always there. Listening to them talk makes me feel more part of a real family than when they speak to me directly ... Because I'm the youngest member of the household, people watch what they say and how they say it in front of me, but when I'm hiding under the table, they usually forget that I'm there and the truth comes out, undisguised, not all "tidied up ..." Those are the moments I wait for ... Right now, all three women in the household are upset—because they don't have enough money to buy a wedding present for Lise Allard, the girl across the street who's getting married soon.

> *He slips under the table and pulls the tablecloth down behind him.*

NANA

We could buy her something for a couple of bucks, but we can't do that, we'd look as poor as we are! It's one thing to be poor, but you can't let it show! The Allards aren't any richer than us, but they manage to hide it so people can act like they don't know. We have to do the same thing. Our present's got to be really gorgeous, to match the really gorgeous present they gave Thérèse when she got married.

ALBERTINE

It wasn't gorgeous at all.

VICTOIRE

It was actually ugly.

NANA

That's not what I mean! You know that! Don't make me waste my breath! Of course it was ugly, but it was expensive, and that's what counts! But we—

VICTOIRE

We can't pretend to be rich with what we've got here on the table!

ALBERTINE

We don't even have enough to pretend that we're poor, for Christ's sake!

> *NANA slaps ALBERTINE on the hand.*

NANA

Don't swear like that, the kid's under the table.

ALBERTINE

If he's old enough to sniff my thighs, he's old enough to hear me swear!

NANA

He's not sniffing your thighs!

ALBERTINE

So what was it that rubbed up against me a while ago? A ghost, maybe? A rat? Mark my words, that kid's going to end up a panty sniffer!

VICTOIRE

Bartine, this is no time for that ...

NANA

Where in heaven's name do you get those expressions, Bartine!? A panty sniffer! It's horrible! You and I sure don't read the same books!

ALBERTINE

Well, my kids aren't the ones who hide under tables listening to what the grownups have to say!

NANA

As if my books were to blame for everything that goes wrong in this house! You should watch what you say! It's impossible to have a real talk around here, we never know where you'll strike next!

VICTOIRE

Stop bickering, the two of you, we'll never solve the problem of Lise Allard's wedding present that way!

ALBERTINE

At least it passes the time! This is the tenth time we've counted the money we don't have!

NANA

Didn't I tell the two of you not to wait ... At the beginning of the week we might've been able to buy her a decent present, but now ... what did you do with your money, for heaven's sake? Seems to me you both had some three days ago!

VICTOIRE

And what did you do with yours? Eh? You had some three days ago, too. Didn't you?

NANA

Well, I came up with more than the two of you!

VICTOIRE

Yeah, fifty cents! Big deal! What can we do with that? Give her ten chocolate bars for her wedding? Stop acting so

holier-than-thou, Nana, find a solution! You're the smart
one in the family, right?

NANA

Why don't you find a solution for once, Madame Tremblay?

VICTOIRE

For once! I'll have you know I raised four kids without your
help! You married one of them, and I don't hear you
complaining about him very often! And I never found one
of my kids under the table spying on the grownups so he
can go yak his head off to everyone in sight!

NANA

Don't tell me you're going to start in now, too! Leave the
poor kid alone! You just told your daughter this was no time
for that.

VICTOIRE

That's true. You're right. As usual.

ALBERTINE

Still, to hear you talk, Nana, it's like you're the only
reasonable one in the family ... Now let's see you prove it
again. I'm exhausted, and besides, I'm just the dummy
around here. So find a way to get us out of this mess and Ma
will be able to sing your praises, as usual. She looks like she's
bawling you out, but it's just an act. Her admiration for you
is boundless! When you're around, she might bawl you out a
bit, but the minute you leave, you should hear her! Nana,
this, Nana, that, next thing you know she'll be lining your
picture up beside the saints at church on Sunday ...

NANA

What's come over you all of a sudden?

VICTOIRE (*uneasy*)

Really ...

ALBERTINE

I'm tired. And I'm sick of counting the same two bucks and
a quarter for hours. Besides, I know that you'll find a
solution, Nana, and that pisses me off! I can already see you
gloating and I can't stand it.

> NANA *pushes back her chair, puts her hand to her heart in a
> grand, dramatic gesture and goes to take refuge in her bedroom.*

13

VICTOIRE

Great, are you happy now? You've made her cry again.

ALBERTINE

What do you, mean—again? As if I spent my days making her cry!

VICTOIRE

You know how sensitive she is, any little thing can upset her—

ALBERTINE

Yeah, and I suppose I'm completely insensitive! What do you think it takes to upset me? The plague? The Third World War? Anyway, she drives me crazy with her martyr act! The minute you raise your voice, she looks all wide-eyed, puts her hand on her heart and you'd think she was headed straight for heaven! A second Virgin Mary! A two-hundred pound ascension!

VICTOIRE

Bartine! She's not that fat!

ALBERTINE

Good thing, too, 'cause they'd need a block and tackle to hoist her up to heaven!

VICTOIRE points beneath the table.

VICTOIRE

Watch what you say ...

ALBERTINE

We always have to watch what we say around here, the damn little spy is always there ... I'm crazy about that kid, I'm his godmother, but sometimes, believe me ...

She starts counting the money again ...

ALBERTINE (*spitefully*)

Maybe we could go without roast beef Saturday night and use the money to buy a wedding present. We could eat mustard sandwiches in honour of Lise Allard!

VICTOIRE

Don't be silly, a roast of beef costs way less than a wedding present!

ALBERTINE

You obviously haven't paid for a roast of beef lately, Ma! I'll show you the bill on Saturday, and you'll see for yourself! (*joking*) Pretty soon, we'll be giving slices of roast beef as wedding presents and the bride and groom will be tickled pink!

She waits to see her mother's reaction to her joke. VICTOIRE doesn't react.

ALBERTINE

You see ... if she had said that, you'd be rolling with laughter on the dining room floor, shouting, stop, stop, I'm going to split a gut.

VICTOIRE

When she cracks a joke, it's funny. What's got into you tonight? Can you tell me? What's this sudden fit of jealousy all about?

ALBERTINE points under the table.

ALBERTINE

Watch out, the big ear is writing this evening's report for his mother!

VICTOIRE (*she shrugs*)

He doesn't know how to write! He hasn't even started school yet!

Long silence.

ALBERTINE stares at her mother.

ALBERTINE

Do I really have to explain that that was just a manner of speaking! And I'm not having a fit of jealousy, I'm rebelling against the injustice of it all.

NANA appears from her bedroom. She is holding an enormous five-pound box of Lowney's chocolates.

ALBERTINE

Good Lord, she's dragged her five-pound box of Lowney's chocolates out from under her bed and she's bringing it to us! This has to be a first! Is she trying to make up for being so smart?

NANA places the box of chocolates on the table.

NANA

Help yourselves.

VICTOIRE

That's your box of chocolates, Nana. Your family bought it on Mother's Day, just for you ...

NANA

I know, but I feel like sharing it today. Chocolate often helps me set my thoughts straight, and believe me, we need to think straight today! If the three of us chew on some chocolate, we might come up with something ...

VICTOIRE (*hand on her heart, stunned*)

You sure, Nana?

NANA gives the box a little shove and it slides over to ALBERTINE's elbow.

NANA

Of course I'm sure! We'll concentrate on what we're eating, instead of screaming at each other, and that'll help. You can't fight when your mouth is full. Look, Bartine, you've got a Bordeaux right there, I know you like those ...

THE NARRATOR comes out from under the table.

ALBERTINE

That kid's not just one big ear, he's got a nose, too!

VICTOIRE

Bartine ... please ...

NANA passes the box of chocolates to ALBERTINE.

NANA

Have one, it will shut you up, it'll prevent you from saying stupid things.

THE NARRATOR

Can I have one, too?

ALBERTINE

We should stuff a couple in his ears.

NANA

Here, sweetheart, have a cherry one.

THE NARRATOR helps himself.

NANA (*to ALBERTINE who has already finished her candy*)

Bartine! I didn't even see you chew it!

ALBERTINE

It had a soft filling. I didn't have to chew long … just crush it with my tongue. Delicious!

NANA

I don't know how you can tell, I'm sure you didn't have time to taste it.

VICTOIRE

Damn, wouldn't you know I'd choose one with a hard centre! It's un-chewable! It's toffee. I've always hated toffee, it gets stuck in your teeth. Just my luck!

NANA

Put it in the ashtray, Madame Tremblay. I'll give you another one … I'll find you one with a soft filling like Albertine's … But don't forget to chew it!

VICTOIRE

You sure? I hate to waste good chocolate like that …

NANA

Don't worry, just put it in the ashtray. Look, here you go, one of the chocolate-covered cherries like Michel's …

THE NARRATOR

It's yummy …

NANA

Of course, it's yummy. But don't even think about it … you're not getting another one.

THE NARRATOR

Why not?

NANA

Because I don't want you to be sick.

THE NARRATOR

I won't be sick …

NANA

When you dig into the chocolate, you're just like me, you've got no will power …

THE NARRATOR

What's will power?

NANA

It's when you can't stop eating chocolate. I don't have any will power. Neither do you.

THE NARRATOR
    Yes, I do ...

> ALBERTINE takes another chocolate from the box and hands it
> to the boy.

ALBERTINE
    When you start debating with him like that, it can go on for
    hours ... Here, take this and go back to your hideout!
    Maybe it smells stronger down there now ... you'll like that.

> THE NARRATOR pounces on the chocolate and goes back under
> the table. The three women concentrate on savouring their
> chocolates for a few seconds.

VICTOIRE
    Tell me, dearie, chewing on my candy just now, I was
    thinking ... am I right that you get four of these boxes of
    candy a year?

NANA
    Well, yes ... for Christmas, for Easter, for Mother's Day and
    for my birthday in September.

VICTOIRE
    And they're just for you, right?

NANA
    Right ... I hide them under my side of the bed so whenever
    I feel like it, I can lean over and take one ... But what are
    you getting at, anyway? You think I don't share them often
    enough?

VICTOIRE
    No, no, it's just that ... has it ever occurred to you ... that
    means you eat twenty pounds of chocolate a year? All by
    yourself.

> ALBERTINE bursts out laughing.

ALBERTINE
    Plus what you eat when we go visiting ... No wonder you're
    fat!

> NANA chokes on her chocolate and coughs into her fist.

NANA
    I brought this out to help us think straight and you rub my
    nose in my twenty pounds of chocolate a year! Is that all the
    thanks I get? You're both heartless. Go ahead and finish the

damn box, and leave me alone! Do you think I have time for this tonight? If we weighed the number of pounds of butter you put on your toast in the morning, Bartine, it would probably make our hair stand on end! You'd be fat too, if you weren't such a bundle of nerves! (*to her mother-in-law*) And if we counted the number of slices of baloney you gobble down when you open the ice box and pretend to be looking for the quart of milk, how many pounds a year do you think it would come to?!

Her hand on her heart, she pushes back her chair.

VICTOIRE

Oh, don't start that again.

ALBERTINE

Don't tell me you're going back to your room!

VICTOIRE

We're just chatting.

ALBERTINE

Saying whatever comes into our heads!

VICTOIRE

We're just chatting to pass the time away.

NANA

Meanwhile, you said it, time is passing and we're no closer to solving our problem! (*ALBERTINE reaches for another chocolate in the box.*) Not that one, it's got a hard centre.

ALBERTINE

I don't think so. I think it's soft …

NANA

I'm telling you, it's hard …

ALBERTINE

We'll see.

She pops the chocolate into her mouth.

NANA

So?

ALBERTINE

I'm going to break a tooth.

NANA

Touch luck. Finish it. Suck on it, it'll keep you busy for a while.

19

She goes to put the box in the china cabinet while the other two women exchange looks. She notices something on one of the shelves.

NANA

Unless ... Maybe I've got an idea ...

VICTOIRE (*visibly reassured*)

What's that?

NANA opens the china cabinet and takes out a green cut-glass dish.

VICTOIRE

Not your beautiful peanut plate!

ALBERTINE

Not your beautiful peanut plate!

THE NARRATOR sticks his head out from under the table.

THE NARRATOR

Not your beautiful peanut plate!

ALBERTINE

How can you?! It's one of the nicest things in the house.

VICTOIRE

You're crazy about it.

THE NARRATOR

You only take it out when we have company.

NANA

Maybe, but we don't have much choice.

VICTOIRE

You can't sacrifice your peanut plate, Nana!

ALBERTINE

It's not worth it. So, they'll know that we're poor, who cares! But we can't give this up just for them!

NANA puts the plate down on the table.

NANA

My sister Béa gave it to me as a wedding present ... That was more than twenty years ago! Boy, did I take good care of that plate! For years, it was the only fancy thing in the house ...

ALBERTINE

Even today … Don't try to find anything that nice in my china …

VICTOIRE

You can't do that, Nana, we'll find something else.

ALBERTINE

Right! I've got a few knickknacks I wouldn't mind getting rid of … Like that dumb doll I got for Christmas, made like a hen to put over the teapot …

VICTOIRE

Thanks a lot, it's nice to know you appreciate our presents!

ALBERTINE (*shrugging*)

Well, not that one!

THE NARRATOR

You can't do that, Mama!

NANA (*to her son*)

Go back to your daydreaming under the table!

ALBERTINE

Daydreaming?

> *ALBERTINE is about to make one of her usual comments but she's dissuaded by a stern look from her mother. THE NARRATOR goes back under the table.*

VICTOIRE

What are you going to tell Béa the next time she comes to visit?

NANA

I'll find something when the time comes. That's the least of my worries right now.

VICTOIRE

A beautiful plate like that doesn't just disappear! People will notice! If you tell Béa you broke it after twenty years, I'm not so sure she'll believe you! Anyway, it's going to leave a big hole in the sideboard!

NANA (*no longer listening to her mother-in-law*)

Now we have to find something to wrap it in.

VICTOIRE

Are you sure you want to do this, Nana?

NANA (*still not listening*)

Oh, I think I know what ...

She goes back to the china cabinet and opens the door at the bottom.

NANA ·

I always keep that kind of thing here ... Don't tell me someone's been nosing around ...

She glances in the direction of THE NARRATOR under the table. VICTOIRE is holding the plate.

VICTOIRE

Just think how many generations of peanuts this plate has seen ... and everybody always finds it beautiful! After all these years, people still tell you, "That plate's really beautiful, Nana ..." Even people who've seen it a hundred times.

ALBERTINE

And you have to admit, there's no wrecking the damn thing! I don't know how many times I've dropped it, it's unbelievable ...

NANA shoots her a look.

ALBERTINE

I didn't always tell you. If I had confessed every time I dropped it doing the dishes, you would've strangled me to death years ago. I bet you wouldn't have let me survive to give birth to my second child.

NANA

We weren't even living under the same roof when your second child was born, Bartine!

ALBERTINE

Well, I almost broke it in your old house, too! Whenever I saw it show up when we were doing the dishes, I wanted to reach for my rosary! One time out of two, the damn thing would slip out of my hands and I could see you strangling me ... And that damn little glass spoon ... I hated that little glass spoon! Just try washing it, it slips through your fingers like a bar of soap and you run around the kitchen like crazy, trying to find it ...

VICTOIRE

And you managed never to break it.

ALBERTINE

I didn't want to end up in a pine box with my hands crossed on my chest, clutching my rosary beads.

NANA comes to the table with an empty box from a boutique called Le Petit Versailles.

NANA

You all make fun of me for keeping the wrapping paper and the boxes from our presents ... Look at this, it's full of the tissue paper I've been keeping for years ... and the plate fits inside perfectly! I'll glue this bow back on, and we're in business ...

NANA wraps the plate in the tissue paper, places it in the box and starts to attach a ribbon.

VICTOIRE

Aren't you going to put some wrapping paper on the box?

NANA (*losing her patience*)

Can I handle this? Please! If you don't mind! Thank you!

VICTOIRE

All right! All right! But it seems to me ... if you're going to give a gift, you may as well make it look pretty ...

NANA

The box comes from Le Petit Versailles, Madame Tremblay! That's fancier than some wrapping paper that would cost an arm and a leg. When they see that, they won't believe how chic it is! They'll say, "Good heavens, a present from Le Petit Versailles! They really went all out for us. How generous of them!" And they'll practically be too embarrassed to open it. Look, doesn't that make a handsome package? You see ... (*She reads, pointing to each syllable.*) *Le Pe-tit Ver-sail-les.* One of the fanciest places in town.

ALBERTINE

Where is *Le Pe-tit Ver-sail-les*, anyway?

NANA

How should I know? It must be in Westmount, for sure!

ALBERTINE

And you think they're going to believe that we went to Westmount to buy their wedding present?

NANA

I don't give a darn what they think, as long as they're surprised when they see the box! (*She sets the box down in the middle of the table and looks at it.*) Look how beautiful it is! I don't want to hear another comment.

> *THE NARRATOR comes out from under the table. He looks at the present.*

THE NARRATOR

What are we going to put our peanuts in now?

NANA

I'll buy another plate that's not so expensive ... with our money for the present ... Besides, it's not the plate that counts, it's the peanuts! I'll pay more for the peanuts and nobody will notice the plate!

ALBERTINE

That's not what you used to say!

NANA

No, but that's what I'm saying today! Because I have no choice! Because we weren't smart enough to save up our money! Because we didn't think ahead!

ALBERTINE

Here we go with the martyr act!

NANA

It's no martyr act. How do you expect me to react to your stupid comments?!

ALBERTINE

Here we go again. It always comes down to that. The minute I open my trap, we all know—

VICTOIRE (*cutting her off to change the subject*)

Would you mind telling me where you got that beautiful box, Nana. Where did it come from? I don't remember ever seeing it before. Did you receive a present from le Petit Versailles?! I think I would've remembered ... The only boxes we ever see around here are from L.N. Messier or maybe Laura Secord ...

ALBERTINE

Don't forget Lowney's!

NANA hesitates a bit before answering.

NANA

Well ... I went to buy some undies at Shiller's once, and I
noticed that box on a shelf behind the counter. I thought it
was really beautiful ... and I knew that it could come in
handy some day, so I asked the salesgirl to put my undies in
it ... And you see, I was right to want it. It's practically saved
our lives today.

*She holds the box tight, without saying a word, and sighs. No
one dares speak.*

NANA (*to her son*)

I'm giving up two precious things at once.

ALBERTINE rolls her eyes.

NANA

Michel, come here ...

He goes over to her.

NANA

You've been under the table ... are your hands dirty?

THE NARRATOR

No ... I don't think so ...

NANA

And you've been eating chocolate, too. Show me your
hands.

*He shows her his hands. She takes a corner of her apron to wipe
them.*

NANA

That'll do.

She fixes his hair the best she can.

NANA

Listen carefully. And then do exactly what I tell you ...
Otherwise you won't have any hands to eat your chocolate
with!

He lowers his head.

NANA

Look me in the eye!

He raises his head.

NANA

Now listen. You're going to take the box, you're going to cross the street and you're going to take it to the Allards' house ...

THE NARRATOR

Aw, Maaaaa!

NANA

There's no, "Aw, Maa" about it! You're going to go down the stairs and across the street, you're going to ring the doorbell and wait for them to answer ... And don't step foot in that house, you understand, just wait till they answer the door! You hear me?!

THE NARRATOR

Yes! I'm not deaf!

NANA

Don't answer back like that! Or I'll give you a fat lip and you'll be lisping for the rest of the day! So! When they come to the door ... Listen carefully ... I know you really like the Allards and you love to hang out at their house, but tonight, you're staying on the balcony! You understand?! No hanging around, you come straight home! When they open the door, you're going to stand up straight, and say, loud and clear, "A wedding present for Mademoiselle Lise Allard." You're going to say it exactly like that, pronouncing every syllable: "A wedding present for Mademoiselle Lise Allard." And once you've handed them the present, you're going to turn around and come home as fast as your little legs can carry you! And if they invite you in, you're going to answer, "The lady who sends the present says she doesn't want me to stay."

THE NARRATOR

Aw, Ma! That's embarrassing!

NANA

"The lady who sends the present says she doesn't want me to stay."

ALBERTINE

They're going to know it's from us, Nana!

NANA

Maybe! But … I don't know … it will be cuter that way, and more … I don't know … more official …

VICTOIRE

Especially since we don't even have a card to include …

NANA (*losing her patience again*)

Honestly! Does anyone have a better idea! C'mon, let's hear it! Otherwise, shut up!

They lower their eyes and look away.

NANA (*turning back to her son*)

If you remember everything I just told you, if you do everything like a good boy, you'll get a couple of chocolates as a reward when you come home … Otherwise, you better go spend the night somewhere else … (*seeing her son's terrified look*) C'mon, I'm just kidding … You know that Mama exaggerates when she talks. Even if you don't do everything I told you, you can sleep here tonight … but I'm warning you, you won't be able to sit on your bottom for days!

She laughs to lighten the mood, but THE NARRATOR hangs his head.

NANA

What's the matter!? It'll be fun! You love playing the little man! And they'll think you're cute! And tomorrow, when you go back to see them … I bet they'll … I don't know, they stuff you with so many goodies when you go to visit, they seem to think we don't feed you!

THE NARRATOR

At least they let me lick the beaters!

NANA

Right! And you feel sick to your stomach when you get home! I've been meaning to say something to them for ages … anyway … In the meantime, go do as I say.

She takes the box away from him.

NANA

But wash your hands first, I don't want to take any chances.

He exits.

ALBERTINE

I hate to say it but I can feel a catastrophe coming on …

VICTOIRE

You're such a defeatist, Bartine …

ALBERTINE

No, I'm a realist … Just you wait and see …

VICTOIRE points to NANA who is holding her box tight.

VICTOIRE

It's not too late to change your mind, Nana …

ALBERTINE

I could sacrifice my teapot dolly made like a hen instead …

NANA

No, it's all right … I've made up my mind … Now that I've made a decision, I can't turn back …

She sighs.

VICTOIRE

But you sure wish you could.

NANA

Yes, I wish I could.

THE NARRATOR returns.

NANA

Did you dry them properly?

THE NARRATOR

Of course, I did …

NANA

I don't want any greasy fingerprints on my box … It's pretty old already …

VICTOIRE

Nana, just give him the damn box so he can deliver it! Otherwise we'll still be discussing it tomorrow night!

NANA

You're right. Go on, sweetheart … and don't forget—

THE NARRATOR

I know, I know … "A wedding present for Mademoiselle Lise Allard …"

NANA

Just remember, it's one of the last times anybody will be calling her Mademoiselle …

THE NARRATOR exits. NANA presses her hand to her heart.

NANA

Good Lord! I hope nothing goes wrong …

ALBERTINE

You want to bet on it?

NANA

You didn't have a cent to contribute to the present, but now you want to make a bet!

ALBERTINE

I don't have anything to bet! But there's no risk … I'm sure to win!

> *NANA glances toward the door.*

NANA

I shouldn't have asked him to do this, I can feel it.

> *She heads for the door of the apartment. The lights go down on the dining room and up on the balcony of the Allards' house. THE NARRATOR rings the doorbell. LISE ALLARD comes to answer the door herself.*

LISE

Oh, it's you, Michel. Come on in.

> *He stays nailed to the spot.*

LISE

Come in … You're not usually so shy when you come to visit …

THE NARRATOR (*too loud and in a forced tone of voice*)

A wed-ding pre-sent for Ma-de-moi-selle Lise Al-lard!

> *He holds out the present.*

LISE

Oh, is that for me! My wedding present! Come in, we'll open it!

THE NARRATOR (*same tone of voice*)

The lady who sent me says she doesn't want me to stay.

> *LISE laughs.*

LISE

Oh, I see … Well, tell her thank you very much.

THE NARRATOR

The same for the others …

LISE

What do you mean, the same for the others ...

THE NARRATOR

The other women who sent me ...

NANA (*who is watching from the other side of the street*)

What on earth is he doing now?

LISE

You'd like to come in, but they don't want you to, is that it?

THE NARRATOR (*same forced tone of voice*)

The lady who sent the present says she doesn't want me to stay!

NANA

What are you waiting for, come back across the damn street!

LISE

Well, I know what we can do ... So you can see me open my present, I'll do it right here on the balcony, with you ...

She starts to open the present.

NANA

What does she think she's doing! It's too dark out, she won't even see that it comes from Le Petit Versailles! She won't even be able to see the present! Great! All that for nothing! I lost my prize possessions for nothing! I sacrificed the nicest thing in the house for nothing!

LISE ALLARD takes the plate out of the box and puts the box down on the balcony, so she can admire the present.

NANA

Look at that! The box is on the ground. She's going to step on it! There'll be nothing left of my beautiful box.

LISE ALLARD raises the plate to eye level.

LISE

Oh, what a beautiful mustard dish.

NANA

Don't say a thing! Don't answer her!

THE NARRATOR

It's not a mustard dish. We always used it for peanuts!

NANA

I'm going to die. I'm going to die of shame! I'm going to give up the ghost right here on my own balcony!

THE NARRATOR realizes what he just said and starts to stutter and stagger …

THE NARRATOR
Uhhhh … no … I mean …

LISE
It's all right … don't faint on me now … it's no big deal … It's a beautiful peanut plate, Michel … A really beautiful peanut plate … (*She looks across the street, realizing that NANA is watching the scene from her balcony.*) Thank you, Madame Tremblay, it's a gorgeous present.

THE NARRATOR turns away, looking miserable.

LISE
Now go see your mother, and tell her how much I love her present.

She closes the door behind her, leaving the box on the balcony.

NANA
To top it off, she'll never know that at least the box came from Le Petit Versailles!

THE NARRATOR heads back toward his mother, dragging his heels.

THE NARRATOR
I didn't do it on purpose, Ma, it just came out by itself …

NANA
I know that …

THE NARRATOR
Are you going to give me a fat lip?

NANA
No. It's not your fault. I should give myself a fat lip … It's true, I always think I'm more reasonable than everyone else … and you see … that's what happens when you get a bright idea and you don't think it through …

THE NARRATOR
So what should you have done?

NANA
I never should've got out of bed! Then I could just lean over the edge and concentrate on my five-pound box of chocolates. That's what everyone says I do best …

She takes him by the hand and leads him back into the now empty dining room. She sits him down on a chair.

NANA

You listened to everything we said a while ago, didn't you?

THE NARRATOR

Well ... I could hear—

NANA

You were listening. How many times have I told you not to lie, a mother knows everything ...

THE NARRATOR

Okay. I was listening ...

NANA

So you see, pride is not for the poor. But sometimes I feel like our pride is all we have left ...

THE NARRATOR

What do you mean? What's *pride?*

NANA

I'd have to read the Larousse Dictionary from cover to cover every morning to answer all your questions.

THE NARRATOR

That's what you always say, and I don't even know what the Larousse Dictionary is.

NANA

It's that fat book we have to consult when you drive us crazy with your questions ...

THE NARRATOR

Grandma's book?

NANA

No, that's an old medical dictionary ... every time your grandmother hears about a disease on the radio, she's sure she's got it so we have to go look it up in her dictionary to prove to her that she's healthy ... No, the Larousse Dictionary is the big book your brother, Coco, is always dragging around ...

THE NARRATOR

The one with all the words in it.

NANA

That's right.

THE NARRATOR
I can hardly wait to read it.

NANA
That makes two of us ... So to get back to pride ... Listen, you just turned six, you'll be starting school in September ... Pretty soon you'll realize that ... I don't know how to explain it ... You'll see that some people have lots of stuff, and others have a lot less, or hardly anything at all ...

THE NARRATOR
I know all that, there's the rich and the poor.

NANA
That's right, the rich and the poor ... And people who are poor like us ... sometimes they don't want it to show ... they don't want other people to know ... they'll do anything to hide it ...

THE NARRATOR
That's what you were talking about before ...

NANA
Yeah ... seems like I've been talking about that a lot lately ... Well, that's what pride is, not wanting other people to know that you're poor ... So they don't make fun of you ... Or because you're ashamed ... It's lots of other things, too, but I think that's enough for tonight ...

THE NARRATOR
Aren't you going to punish me?

NANA
If you see Madame Allard and her daughters laugh when we walk by on our way to Mass next Sunday, just remember that I'm the one who's being punished ...

THE NARRATOR
They won't laugh at us ...

NANA
What?

THE NARRATOR
Madame Allard and her daughters won't laugh at us.

NANA
Oh, no?

THE NARRATOR

No.

NANA

Why not?

THE NARRATOR

Because it's not funny.

Brief silence. NANA sighs.

NANA

It's not funny for us, but it might be funny for other people.

THE NARRATOR

That's not fair.

NANA

No, you're right, it's not fair ... Listen ... imagine us walking
by them, and they laugh ... Can you imagine it?

THE NARRATOR

Yes ...

NANA

How do you feel?

THE NARRATOR

I feel bad. I'm ashamed ... And I hate it ...

NANA

Well, feeling ashamed proves that you have your pride, boy
... So now, it's time for you to go to bed ...

THE NARRATOR

I guess I haven't earned my chocolates ... ?

NANA

No, you certainly haven't earned your chocolates tonight.

*They head for the bedroom, hand in hand. THE NARRATOR
comes back.*

THE NARRATOR

A few days later, my mother received a thank you note from
Lise Allard: "Many thanks to you all for the lovely nut server.
We will think of you whenever we use it."

Nana returns.

NANA

She means, they'll make fun of us whenever they use it ...
Maybe you don't realize it, you poor kid, but you've started
a legend they'll pass down for generations ... That dish'll to

be famous in the Allard family till the end of time! (*She blows her nose and wipes her eyes.*) Anyway, somebody snobbish enough to call that plate a "lovely nut server" didn't deserve any better!

    She exits.

VICTOIRE (*offstage*)

    Great, there's another thunderstorm on its way! We're going to spend another sleepless night!

THE NARRATOR

    My grandmother never liked thunderstorms.

    VICTOIRE enters, wearing her nightclothes.

VICTOIRE

    It's not that I never liked them, I always HATED thunderstorms.

THE NARRATOR

    Why, Grandma?

VICTOIRE

    I don't know. I guess it's because it's the closest I've ever come to death.

THE NARRATOR

    Death is when someone goes away forever, right?

VICTOIRE

    Did your mother tell you that?

THE NARRATOR

    Yes. She said that it was like that time we found Itty-Bitty at the bottom of his cage …

VICTOIRE

    That's your mother for you … using the death of a canary as a way of explaining death to her son!

THE NARRATOR

    Isn't it true?

VICTOIRE

    Oh, yes, it's true.

THE NARRATOR

    But why do you say that thunderstorms make you think of death?

VICTOIRE

Because in the middle of the storms, there's fire, and fire always makes me think of death.

THE NARRATOR

Are you afraid of going to hell?

VICTOIRE looks at THE NARRATOR.

VICTOIRE

I hope your mother didn't tell you that my poor Itty-Bitty could've gone to Hell!

THE NARRATOR

Of course, she didn't.

VICTOIRE

That would be just like her ... Anyway ... A thunderstorm soaks everything too fast, it can ruin a harvest in the blink of an eye, it makes a racket, and ... there's always the risk that the goshdarn ball of fire will strike.

THE NARRATOR

Oh, yeah! Tell me the story of the ball of fire!

VICTOIRE

You love it when we tell you scary stories, don't you?

THE NARRATOR

That story isn't scary, it makes me laugh.

VICTOIRE

Well, believe you me, young man, if you'd been there, you wouldn't have laughed. And it only makes you laugh, because I make it funny ... Listen ... I hadn't been married long when it happened ... We'd just moved to Montreal and I still wasn't used to being in a big city ...

THE NARRATOR smiles broadly and settles down to listen to the story.

THE NARRATOR

You were in the middle of doing your ironing ...

VICTOIRE

That's right. But don't interrupt me when I'm talking, it makes me lose my train of thought ... I'd put my three irons on the woodstove—I'd received three of them as wedding presents and that was really practical ... when one of them got cold, I still had two hot ones—there were no electric

36

irons in those days, we couldn't just plug something into the wall and expect it to light up or get hot like magic! I'm telling you, women today don't realize how spoiled they are ... Anyway, I was in middle of ironing one of your grandfather's shirts ... I'd started on the collar ... you have to be careful with the collar, you got to get it right, it has to be perfect, because that's what everybody notices first ... I was concentrating so hard on my collar, I forgot to close the front door and the one in the back at the opposite end of the hall ... In the country, I did it automatically, but here in the city, I'd never seen any bad thunderstorms ... I knew there was a storm on its way, it was pitch black outside in the middle of the afternoon, and it was awful muggy ... I knew that, but ... I guess I was too preoccupied with my collar. Or maybe I thought there was no such thing as a bad storm in the city ... only in the country ... Then all of a sudden ... All of a sudden ... This is what you were waiting for, right?

THE NARRATOR
Yes, yes, yes ... Then all of sudden ...

VICTOIRE
All of sudden, kid ...

    THE NARRATOR smiles, delighted.

VICTOIRE
Kababoom! Kaboom! Kabow! (*to* THE NARRATOR) Is that loud enough for you?

THE NARRATOR
No. Louder!

VICTOIRE
KABABOOM! KABOOM! KABOW! It scared the living daylights out of me! My heart was in my throat, I must've jumped a foot off the ground and I almost burned myself with the iron—

THE NARRATOR
That's new ...

VICTOIRE
What?

THE NARRATOR
The iron, that's new ...

VICTOIRE

Hey, what do you want, a story or the truth?

THE NARRATOR

Well ... both.

VICTOIRE

Both is impossible. Not if you want it to be interesting. So you have to choose.

THE NARRATOR

All right, then, the story ...

VICTOIRE

That's more like it. But now you've interrupted me so much, you won't be scared and you won't laugh either.

THE NARRATOR

You're right, I might not be scared, but I'll laugh ... I promise!

VICTOIRE begins a pantomime that delights her grandson.

VICTOIRE

Then ... I hardly had time to turn around and I saw ... I saw a ball of fire the size of the living room sofa and as red as the heart of the woodstove in the middle of January come rolling through the front door, cross the whole house, the whole house, you hear me, burning everything in its path, then out it went through the back door, as if it had seen what it came to see! It only lasted maybe two seconds, but those were the longest two seconds in my life! I raced to close both doors before it decided to come back ... I don't know how I did it ... The hair was standing up on my arms and the hair on my head was so frizzy, it looked like it'd spent the night in rags!

THE NARRATOR laughs.

VICTOIRE

Good! Hallelujah! I made him laugh! Amazing! Well, there was a scorch mark on the floor, it looked like a three-hundred pound iron had been forgotten in the middle of the house! A scorch mark as big as the house! I'd had a brush with death that time, young man, and ever since, every time I hear that a storm's on its way, I get out my palm leaves and my rosary beads and my holy water and I lock myself up in the closet!

THE NARRATOR
    That makes me laugh, too!
VICTOIRE
    What does?
THE NARRATOR
    When you all go to hide in the closets, you and Mama and
    aunt Albertine ...
VICTOIRE
    If the ball of fire comes into the house, it'll never come
    knocking on the closet door in my bedroom! So I know I'm
    safe!
THE NARRATOR
    Papa says the three of you are putting on an act, that you
    exaggerate ... and you're not really that scared ...
VICTOIRE
    Your father might be my son, but believe you me, sometimes
    he's a bit short on the grey matter.
THE NARRATOR
    What's grey matter?
VICTOIRE
    It's what you've got between your ears ... (*with a sly smile*)
    And sometimes all your father's got between his ears is one
    big gap! So, go to bed now, let me get out my palm leaves
    and my holy water ...
THE NARRATOR
    But you still haven't explained what death is ... When
    someone goes away, where do they go? Heaven and Hell and
    all that, I don't understand ...
VICTOIRE
    You're too young for that stuff ... Because it could scare you,
    for real ... Let's just say ... let's say my suitcase has been
    packed for ages now, so when it's time for me to leave—
THE NARRATOR
    I've been in your closet lots of times, and there's no
    suitcase—

VICTOIRE

It's a manner of speaking. Itty-Bitty didn't pack his suitcase either ... Hey, do you mind telling me what you do in my closet?

THE NARRATOR

Sometimes I pretend there's a thunderstorm and I run to hide there ...

VICTOIRE

I hope you don't use my beautiful palm leaves!

THE NARRATOR hangs his head.

VICTOIRE

I know one ball of fire that could find you at the back of the closet, kid. A ball of fire with a black dress and grey hair. And it won't be your hair that's frizzy, it'll be your bum! You'll have to sleep on your stomach for the rest of the week, and eat standing up beside the table!

THE NARRATOR (*to change the subject*)

If you haven't packed a suitcase, Grandma, does that mean you won't be going very far?

VICTOIRE

All I know is, it's not far away in time ...

THE NARRATOR

What does that mean?

VICTOIRE (*after a moment's reflection*)

That means that one of these fine days, maybe sooner than we think, you'll get up and find out that Grandma's gone ... It'll make you sad, for sure, but I don't want you all bothered about it for too long ... When it happens ... when it happens, you have my permission to cry a little, for sure, but not too much ... Tell yourself that Grandma hasn't gone very far, she didn't even need a suitcase, and wherever she is, she's happy at last ...

THE NARRATOR

What do you mean, at last? Aren't you happy with us?

She goes over to him and caresses his face.

VICTOIRE

A long time from now, when you're much older, you might learn things about your grandmother that will shock you.

But just remember that for the short while it lasted, your grandmother was very happy ... And there's no price too high to pay for that kind of happiness ...

THE NARRATOR

I don't understand ...

VICTOIRE

I know. And maybe I shouldn't tell you all that today, but ... (*She moves her face closer to his.*) I might be leaving sooner than we think, and I wouldn't want it to take you by surprise ... There's nothing terrible about leaving for that place where you don't need a suitcase once you're ready ... And your Grandma's been ready for a long time now ... Don't forget that when you find out that I'm gone.

NANA enters, also wearing her nightclothes.

NANA

Honestly, Madame Tremblay! Scaring a child like that just before I put him to bed! At your age! You're like a school girl! Sometimes I swear you act younger than him! Now I'm the one who has to un-upset him, as usual!

VICTOIRE

There's nothing that child likes better than being scared! Besides, he's the one who asked for it.

NANA

He asked you to scare him!

VICTOIRE

That's right.

NANA (*to her son*)

You asked her to scare you.

THE NARRATOR

Well ... yes.

NANA (*as she exits*)

In that case, you can put him to bed, I wash my hands of the whole matter ... Really, sometimes, I don't know ...

VICTOIRE (*loud enough for NANA to hear her*)

We're supposed to be living in a temperate climate, but I'm telling you, people's attitudes are like the weather— extreme! (*to THE NARRATOR*) A temperate climate, my eye! I read that again in this morning's paper—we're so lucky to live in a temperate climate! Temperate! Honestly! The winter's too cold and the summer's too hot, the winter's too long, the summer's too short, spring is too muddy and the fall is depressing ... Personally, I'd be happy with the month of May or the month of September all year long! They say it was September year round in the Garden of Eden! They never ran out of fresh fruit and vegetables. They could eat corn on the cob and cooked beets with lots of butter all year! Imagine! Adam and Eve had fresh produce twelve months of the year, the lucky stiffs! It was always apple season ... And I guess that was their downfall. It just goes to show you, eh? (*She laughs at her own joke, but THE NARRATOR doesn't get it.*) We go nuts and work our bums off trying to prepare enough food for the rest of the year during the three short weeks when fresh fruit and vegetables are available! The whole house smells of ketchup and relish! It smells so good it brings tears to your eyes! And that's how I wish it smelled all year! But, unfortunately, in this part of the world, the month of September only lasts four weeks. Which reminds me that your mother was born on September 2nd, and that means that the day of her birth, it was the same temperature as in the Garden of Eden! I never thought about that! Lucky woman!

THE NARRATOR (*amazed*)
Huh!

NANA (*who stayed nearby to listen*)
Madame Tremblay! Honestly! A woman who reads as much as you can't believe such nonsense! You shouldn't put things like that into his head, he'll end up believing you! Besides, I'd like to know who went to check that out! Was there a weatherman in the Garden of Eden? Is it written in the Bible? "And God invented the month of September and He saw that it was good." You're too intelligent to believe that!

VICTOIRE
You know we're not allowed to read the Bible! So I can't go see for myself. And besides they say it's written in a language we couldn't understand ...

NANA

Thank heavens, because there'd be no end to the tales you'd tell. You come up with some winners, just with the New Testament—

VICTOIRE (*cutting her off*)

Well, I guess I'm like you, dearie. I believe what suits me!

NANA

But you don't have to put stuff like that into the kid's head!

VICTOIRE goes over to NANA and looks her in the eye.

VICTOIRE

The day you prove to me that you haven't put anything into that child's head, I'll apologize. Not before.

Loud thunderclap. It starts to rain. The lights go out.

VICTOIRE

Oh, my God! The storm!

NANA

Close the windows, everybody!

ALBERTINE (*offstage*)

It's the end of the world!

Thunder. Rain.

NANA

I never heard anything like it!

ALBERTINE (*offstage*)

My bed is already soaking wet!

NANA

Impossible! It just started to rain.

Lightning.

Thunder.

Albertine enters, also wearing her nightclothes.

ALBERTINE

Did you see that? I thought someone was taking our picture! And Ma has disappeared! She's not in her closet!

VICTOIRE (*searching through a cupboard*)

I'm right here, Bartine, I'm looking for my holy stuff ... Here, both of you, light yourselves a candle and go into your closets with these palm leaves ... And take the kids with you ... But don't set the house on fire ...

During the pandemonium, GABRIEL enters and sits down in his mother's rocking chair. The three women exit amid the thunder and lightning.

ALBERTINE (*offstage*)

I'm coming to hide in your closet with you, Ma, I'm too scared!

VICTOIRE

My closet's too small.

ALBERTINE

Just push over ...

VICTOIRE

I thought I told you to go hide in a closet with your kids!

GABRIEL smiles. THE NARRATOR goes over to him.

GABRIEL

You see how they love being in a tizzy!

ALBERTINE

If the ball of fire comes in the house, it'll get caught inside and kill us all! Everything's shut tight, it'll never get out!

VICTOIRE

If everything's shut tight, it can't get in, you ninny! Shut up!

NANA (*coming back from their bedroom*)

Go see if everything's all right in the rest of the house, Gabriel, I'm going into the closet.

ALBERTINE

Help! I dropped my candle in my bed! I dropped my candle in my bed! Oh, no, there it is! My candle went out! My candle went out!

THE NARRATOR

I want to go with you, Mama ...

NANA

Don't worry, you'll be fine in your bed ... it's right beside the closet so I won't be far ... (*glancing at GABRIEL*) You see, sometimes it's practical to have your bed in our room ... But, wait a minute, how come you're not asleep?

THE NARRATOR

The noise woke me up.

GABRIEL

And I'm sure it wasn't the thunder that woke him up, it's all of you.

NANA

Very funny! In the meantime, make yourself useful! Make sure that nothing in the house is open a crack!

She exits. GABRIEL stands up and goes over to THE NARRATOR's armchair.

GABRIEL

Are you in your bed, Michel? I can't see you in the dark.

THE NARRATOR

Of course I am.

GABRIEL

Are you still scared?

Thunder and lightning at the same time.

THE NARRATOR

Yes.

GABRIEL

Don't be scared. It's not true that it's dangerous. You're not answering me? Don't you believe me?

THE NARRATOR simply shakes his head no.

GABRIEL

Come on, I'll prove to you that it's not dangerous.

NANA

Gabriel, I'm warning you ...

GABRIEL (*smiling*)

You just stay in your hiding place, Nana, while we have a man-to-man talk. You should see yourself. You look like a bear gone to hibernate in our closet! All I can see is a big pale bump ... (*smiling*) that's trembling. Leave the kid with me for once, he's always tied to your apron strings!

NANA

Oh, no, I know you ... you're up to no good ...

GABRIEL (*to his son*)

Come make the rounds of the house with me ...

NANA

Gabriel ...

45

GABRIEL (*tickling THE NARRATOR*)

C'mon!

THE NARRATOR (*struggling*)

Papa, that tickles!

GABRIEL

You'll see, there's nothing to be afraid of.

He makes the gesture of taking a child into his arms. THE NARRATOR lets out a little squeal of surprise.

NANA

I'm warning you, if you electrocute my son, I don't know what I'll do to you!

THE NARRATOR

I'm up so high! I'm up so high!

GABRIEL

You sure are! Six feet up plus my arms ... Watch your head ...

THE NARRATOR follows him, ducking his head. The power comes back at that point.

ALBERTINE

Good Lord! There's too much 'lectricity! The lights are going to explode.

THE NARRATOR

I'm as high as the globe on the dining room ceiling!

GABRIEL

You want to touch it?

THE NARRATOR

Wow! I'm touching it! I'm touching it, Ma! I'm touching the globe on the dining room ceiling!

NANA

You better watch out for your own little globes! You might fall from up there and land on them hard!

THE NARRATOR

Yuck! It's dirty! It's all sticky and covered in brown grease. And full of dead flies!

NANA

Tell your father, that's supposed to be his job!

GABRIEL

C'mon, let's go explore the rest of the house, we'll see if can
find a ball of fire hiding somewhere.

Thunderclap. The lights go out again.

ALBERTINE (*offstage*)

I told you!

GABRIEL puts his son on his shoulders.

GABRIEL

Wow, you weigh a ton!

THE NARRATOR

That's because it's been a long time since you held me in
your arms!

GABRIEL

You're not a baby anymore, Michel.

THE NARRATOR (*quietly*)

I know, but I like it anyway.

GABRIEL

What?

THE NARRATOR

Nothing. Gee, is this how you grownups see the world? From
up high like this? Doesn't it make you dizzy?

GABRIEL laughs.

GABRIEL

Sometimes I'd like to see the world from under the dining
room table! There must be some pretty interesting bits. Eh?
Duck your head, we're going into the kitchen.

THE NARRATOR

Oh! The table looks so small! And you can reach the box of
cookies on the ice box! Lucky you!

GABRIEL

No ball of fire in the stove?

THE NARRATOR (*laughing*)

Nope! No ball of fire in the stove!

*GABRIEL runs across the stage, THE NARRATOR shrieks gleeful-
ly.*

THE NARRATOR

I feel like I'm flying! Everything looks so small and
everything's moving too fast!

GABRIEL

Your grandma's room … let's scare her! Kababoom! Kapow! Kapapow!

VICTOIRE

You scared the wits out of me, you big empty jug!

GABRIEL

Not too much damage, Ma? Did the ball of fire scorch your derrière?

VICTOIRE

Stop that nonsense! How would you like to spend the night with your nose in the mothballs?

GABRIEL (*to his son*)

Looks like she's still alive. Oh, well, maybe next time.

THE NARRATOR laughs.

VICTOIRE

Michel! I forbid you to laugh at dumb jokes like that!

The biggest thunderclap of all strikes.

GABRIEL

Oh, boy! That was a beauty! Let's go see what it's like outside.

ALBERTINE (*offstage*)

Oh, my God! Did somebody say something? I'm deaf!

GABRIEL (*to his son*)

Stop squirming like that, Michel, we're going to watch one of the greatest shows on earth.

GABRIEL and THE NARRATOR are on the balcony overlooking Fabre Street.

Rain, thunder, lightning.

THE NARRATOR stands just behind his father, a bit like in a duet at the opera.

GABRIEL

Look at that, Michel. Isn't that beautiful?!

THE NARRATOR

I can't see a thing!

GABRIEL

What do you mean, you can't see a thing?

THE NARRATOR
   My eyes are closed!
GABRIEL
   Well, open them!
THE NARRATOR
   I can't ...
GABRIEL
   Sure you can, c'mon ...
THE NARRATOR
   No, I can't.
GABRIEL
   Yes, you can. C'mon now. Open one of them ... just a bit at
   first ...
THE NARRATOR
   No.
GABRIEL
   Then stretch out your arms, at least ... to feel the rain.
      Slowly, THE NARRATOR stretches his arms out over GABRIEL's
      shoulders.
GABRIEL
   You feel the rain?
THE NARRATOR
   Yes ... it's warm ... it's warm water!
GABRIEL
   Have you opened your eyes?
THE NARRATOR
   No, not yet ...
GABRIEL
   Open them ... just a little bit ... c'mon, give it a try ...
      As THE NARRATOR gradually opens his eyes, the concert in the
      heavens continues. GABRIEL leans forward a bit.
THE NARRATOR
   Oh! It's true! It is beautiful! And it's pouring rain on my
   head! (*He lifts up his head and opens his mouth.*) Papa! I can
   drink the rain!
      GABRIEL smiles.

GABRIEL

Now you can't say I never showed you anything …

*THE NARRATOR withdraws his arms, GABRIEL stands up
straight. The storm begins to die down.*

THE NARRATOR

Is it true that the Good Lord is angry?

GABRIEL

Don't be silly! You shouldn't believe stuff like that.

THE NARRATOR

That's what Grandma says …

GABRIEL

Grandma also says that water from Easter Sunday can cure a
stomach ache, and that her damn palm leaves can ward off
the Devil. Your grandmother explains everything with the
Good Lord … don't pay attention to her …

THE NARRATOR

So what is it, if it's not Him?

GABRIEL

It's Nature. Nature, that's all.

THE NARRATOR

Is Nature mad?

GABRIEL

I don't know if Nature's mad, but I can tell you, there's
nothing more beautiful or more powerful than Nature.
Never forget that! Nothing! My father's the one … (*He
corrects himself.*) My uncle Josaphat's the one who showed me
that when I was little in Duhamel … He did the same thing I
just did with you, he took me out onto the porch during a
big thunderstorm, and I've never forgotten it. A storm is the
greatest show on earth and you shouldn't run away from it.
Don't go hiding in closets! There's nothing but the dark in
closets! The dark and ignorance and fear. Here on the
balcony, in the middle of the storm … it's … I don't know
… it's powerful … and it sets you free. You just raise your
arms in the middle of all that noise and light and rain, and
it feels good. I think it cleanses you!

*They both smile. THE NARRATOR places his hands on
GABRIEL's shoulders.*

50

GABRIEL
   You see, it's almost over, and nothing happened to us. The
   storm is moving off …
THE NARRATOR
   That's too bad …
GABRIEL
   We should go in now …
THE NARRATOR
   I guess so …
GABRIEL
   I don't feel like it … how 'bout you?
THE NARRATOR
   Me neither.
GABRIEL
   So let's stay here a bit longer …
THE NARRATOR
   Okay.
GABRIEL
   Until your mother comes to get us …
THE NARRATOR
   Okay.

   *THE NARRATOR puts his arms around GABRIEL's neck, presses
   his forehead into his shoulder and cries.*
   Music.
   BLACKOUT

Act Two

THE NARRATOR

Every year, as the holidays approach, a gentle madness descends on the household. It begins with the smell of fresh apple pie—something we eat only once a year and we go crazy stuffing ourselves with those pies. Then comes the smell of fresh doughnuts—my grandmother, my mother and my aunt make them by the dozen and their doughnuts are famous throughout the family. Then, a few days before Christmas, the Christmas tree makes its appearance. (*An undecorated Christmas tree appears in the bow window of the dining room.*) My father and brothers always buy the biggest, the fullest, the most beautiful tree they can find. Half of the time we have to chop off the top because the tree's too tall. My mother uses those branches to decorate the dinner table on Christmas Eve. And two days before Christmas, the ritual of decorating the tree begins. It's always complicated, chaotic and often pretty crazy, but it's one of my favourite moments of the year. (*NANA enters carrying four or five boxes of Christmas tree decorations. Throughout the following scene, she will take the ornaments out of the boxes and attach a little metal hook to each one. For the time being, she simply puts the boxes down on the table. Then she sits down. THE NARRATOR comes to sit in the chair facing his mother.*) But this year—the year I turned six—I have a problem I'm afraid I won't be able to explain to my mother ... Because I need money. And she's impossible when it comes to money. Because she doesn't have any. (*He lets out a huge sigh and launches in:*) Mamaaaaa ...

NANA

When you start bleating like that, I know you're going to ask me for something ... Now what is it?

THE NARRATOR
Well, it's for school …

NANA
Not again!

THE NARRATOR
Why do you say, not again?

NANA
Because I can tell it's going to cost me money … Funny how when it's for school, I always have to reach for my purse! So, Michel, is it going to cost me money?

THE NARRATOR
Well … yes …

NANA
I knew it! Now what's the deal? Are they selling Baby Jesus lollipops for Christmas? Does the priest need new underwear? Have the sisters run out of wimples?

THE NARRATOR (*smiling despite himself*)
C'mon! The sisters never ask us for money for stuff like that …

NANA
Well, they sure ask us for money for everything else! Sometimes I feel like we buy their toilet paper and their bath oil! What was the last thing … The canonization of that crazy woman who saw saints everywhere? Well, now … thanks to my money, she's part of her own vision! But that was at least a month ago. Now what is it? A life-size Christmas manger? The missions in China?

THE NARRATOR
Yes, it's for the missions in China …

NANA
Here we go again! Every year at Christmas, they hit us with the missions in China! After the holidays, there's a white sale at Dupuis Frères, and before the holidays, the Chinese go on sale at Saint-Stanislas-de-Koska Church! How can they get away with it? Just two weeks ago, they were asking for money to cure Lord-knows-who of yellow fever or the tse-tse fly, I can't remember … Leave it to them to think that money can cure yellow fever! Those missionaries should stay home and catch a good old-fashioned flu like the rest of us!

It would cost us less and I'd have more money for my
Christmas presents!

THE NARRATOR

Listen, Ma ...

NANA

I'm listening ...

THE NARRATOR

You're not listening, you keep talking ...

NANA

I might interrupt you a bit, but I'm listening ...

THE NARRATOR

It's because—

NANA

Oh, I'm sure there's a good reason—

THE NARRATOR

There is a good reason!

NANA

Go ahead, I'm listening ... I'll bite my tongue ...

THE NARRATOR

You know ... I already told you that they gave us all a pretty
drawing of an airplane, with a hundred little cut-out
windows ... And every time we buy a Chinese kid, we get to
fill in a window with any colour we want—

NANA

You must've filled in two hundred airplane pictures since
the school year began! Honestly, haven't they run out of
them yet?!

THE NARRATOR

Very funny—

NANA

I'm not so sure I was joking, Michel ...

THE NARRATOR

Anyway, because it's Christmas, we get to fill in *two* windows
for every dime we bring in.

NANA

My God! How generous can they get?! They're going to go
bankrupt! (*Change of tone.*) I told you—they're holding a
sale! A clearance sale, offering two Chinese kids for the

price of one! They'd stoop to anything to collect our money!

THE NARRATOR

Maybe, but I only have twenty more windows to fill in!

NANA

A dollar! You dare come ask me for a dollar to buy twenty Chinese kids a few days before Christmas! Do you realize what a dollar means to us? Do you? Do the brothers and the sisters realize what it means to us? I can feed a household of twelve people with a dollar, Michel! I can produce a feast with a dollar! A wedding banquet!

THE NARRATOR

C'mon!

NANA

You'd be surprised what I can do with one measly dollar, young man! There are days when it's a miracle what shows up in your plate, for the price I paid! You can go see that teaching brother who smelled to high heaven at the last parent-teachers meeting, and tell him that your mother is going to feed her own children before she buys you some Chinese kids for Christmas, even if they're on sale!

THE NARRATOR

You're not buying Chinese kids *for me*, Mama, they're not toys. You're buying Chinese kids to save their *souls*. That's different.

NANA

To save their souls! Is that what they tell you at school? Well, believe me, that's not the way you've been talking about them since September. You've been buying Chinese children by the barrelful since you went back to school, and you call them all Michel. Sometimes it feels like half the population of China is named Michel. Honestly! When you talk about them, you make it sound like they really belong to you. Not their souls that were saved, oh, no, but them, themselves. Just like they were your playthings! You show everyone their pictures and say, "Look, these are my Chinese children! They're all named Michel Tremblay!"

THE NARRATOR

They're not named Michel Tremblay. Just Michel.

NANA

Oh, yeah? Michel Wong? Michel Chang? You're going to
celebrate your First Communion soon. I can't believe you
still think that you can really buy Chinese children to save
their souls! It's about time you stopped believing in stuff like
that!

THE NARRATOR

So what am I buying when they tell me it's Chinese
children?

NANA

How do I know? I was just kidding a while ago, but maybe
I'm not so far off ... Maybe it's true that you're buying
wimples for the nuns ... Or underwear for the priests. Those
people never pay for anything themselves! They get
everything free ... including the best locations for their big,
beautiful churches ... without paying a damn penny in taxes!
And they don't pay income tax either! They've got one heck-
uva nerve coming to ask poor people like us to tighten our
belts at Christmas time to buy more Chinese kids, closing
sale prices or not! Do you believe that stuff, Michel? Well, I
don't, you hear me, I don't believe a word of it!

THE NARRATOR

Ma!!!!

NANA

What? Do you follow that money? Do you know where it
ends up, for real? Does it really take a boat to China, or
does it land in the sisters' dresser drawers?

THE NARRATOR

Nuns aren't liars!

NANA

Nuns were invented to make up lies, Michel!

THE NARRATOR

That's not true!

NANA

And they're prepared to do anything to fill their pockets.
When they see a quarter, their veils start quivering and their
tongues hang out a good six inches. They drool over a
quarter like your grandmother's cat used to drool over the
birdcage when Itty-Bitty was still alive! The nuns and the

brothers, and the priests, too, for that matter ... I bet their suppers are a heckuvalot more interesting the weeks when they put the pressure on you to buy as many Chinese kids as possible! Your money probably lands in their plates, Michel. Maybe it turns into hamburger meat and canned corn!

THE NARRATOR

Don't say that!

NANA

You're right. I probably shouldn't say that to a child ... but the whole business drives me crazy, if you only knew ...

THE NARRATOR

It's true that the sisters have missions in China! They showed us a movie.

NANA

Of course, it's true. I know that ... I've seen those movies, they used to show them when I was a little girl in the back of beyond in Saskatchewan! Silent movies with priests parading around and the Chinese working as their porters! And believe you me, it wasn't Chinese souls that were carrying their packages! And it didn't look like there was a lot of religion between them either. The day I see a priest carry a package for a Chinaman, maybe I'll start to believe them. But not before! Can you please tell me what they think they're doing there, for God's sake! Saving souls! Hmmph! There are souls to be saved right here. I'd be happy to show them a few! Why can't they leave the poor Chinese in peace? They already have a religion, seems to me one's enough!

THE NARRATOR

But it's not the right one! If they don't become Catholics, they'll go straight to Hell!

NANA

Then it's going to be crowded in Hell! There are six hundred million of them, Michel. There won't be any room left for us! Six hundred million! Don't tell me the nuns think they can send three priests and ten nuns to convert six hundred million people! That's a big job! It'll take a lot of airplane pictures!

THE NARRATOR

They send more missionaries than that!

NANA

Sure. Let's say twice as many! But never enough to convert all of China! Wake up! Did they manage to convert all the Indians when they arrived here? No! They had to kill them to make them think like them! And there were a lot less Indians than there are Chinese in China!!

THE NARRATOR

Ma!!!

NANA

They should hire me to teach Canadian history! You'd all be in for a few surprises!

THE NARRATOR

Okay, forget the whole thing ...

NANA

Wait a minute. I didn't say you could leave the table! Listen to me ... I haven't finished ... I don't want you to be ashamed of me because I refuse to give you a dollar to buy twenty Chinese children ... As if you could buy people!

THE NARRATOR

I told you, it's their souls—

NANA

That's even worse! How can they put things like that into a child's head! What are they thinking of?! The population of China is ten times bigger than ours, Michel! It would serve the priests right if some day the Chinese decided to come here to buy some French Canadian kids! Can you picture that ... a bunch of Chinese nuns arriving to convert us all? Who's their God, again? Buddha? Can you see yourself forced to believe in Buddha who you don't know from Adam and Eve? Put yourself in their place ... we show up in their country with stories they've never heard, and we start selling their kids to ours ... No wonder they hate us!

THE NARRATOR

But we're the ones who are right! We're the ones who have the true faith!

NANA

That's what those little Chinese kids you buy are being told,
too! Did you ever think of that?

THE NARRATOR

Maybe, but they don't know that they don't have the true
faith! We have to tell them!

NANA

Maybe there's a little Chinese boy having this same
conversation with his mother over a bowl of won ton soup
right now. And his mother is saying the same thing as me ...
Maybe she's right for them, and I'm right for us ... Why
should we try to force other people to think like us?

THE NARRATOR

But that's what you always try to do ...

NANA

Don't get smart with me, young man! You know I love a
good discussion ... but that doesn't mean I really want you
to think like me, Michel ... I'm not going to act like the
nuns, I won't force you to believe what I'm saying ... you can
go on believing the sisters, and the brothers and the priests,
if you want ... but don't count on me to subsidize their
fancy Saturday night suppers!

THE NARRATOR

Ma!!!

NANA

Like it or not, that's how it is.

THE NARRATOR

So what am I going to say? I can't tell them my mother
doesn't want to give me the money because she's sure it'll
end up in their plates!

NANA

You've got a point there ... I guess you're the one who has
to spend the rest of the year with them ... You see, they
don't even have to blackmail me, I do it to myself!

THE NARRATOR

What's blackmail?

NANA

Never mind. You'll find out soon enough. (*Noticing her son's
insistent look.*) Blackmail is what you do when you threaten to

go on a hunger strike if I try to hide chunks of turnip in your potatoes! Listen, I don't know what to say now ...

THE NARRATOR (*smiling*)

That's rare ...

NANA

Right, it's rare, but it happens, and I'm embarrassed ...

THE NARRATOR

Does that mean I'm going to get my money?

NANA

You're going to get your money, but I want to make something clear ... I'm not giving you the money because I believe in their nonsense. You hear me. I'm doing it so they leave you alone ... I don't want them treating you like a poor kid, like a beggar, even if it's almost true. I don't want people making fun of you, and they just might do it. I don't want to spoil your First Communion. I'm buying peace for you, Michel, that's what I'm doing. You understand?

THE NARRATOR

No.

NANA

I know you don't. I just hope you'll understand some day. In the meantime, I'll buy your little slanty-eyed Michel Tremblays for you. Since it looks like there's no way around it ... I'll give you fifty cents, you can buy ten of them ... And we'll see after your Christmas vacation if we have enough money to save another ten souls ...

THE NARRATOR

But that means my picture won't be finished for Christmas! There's only one day left of school!

NANA

You can tell the brother who's teaching you that our Christmas turkey is going to weigh two pounds less because of this, and I can't buy one that weighs four pounds less 'cause there wouldn't be enough food to feed the whole family ...

THE NARRATOR walks away, hanging his head. NANA catches up with him and puts her hand on his shoulder.

NANA

Don't tell him that for real.

THE NARRATOR

I won't tell him if you give me the rest of the money.

She shoos him away, with some slaps on his bum. He leans against the table.

NANA

You learn fast, you little rascal! (*She smoothes her hair and adjusts her apron.*) If only the others would arrive, we could start decorating the darn tree ... My decorations are almost ready ... Look, I found the bird of paradise I lost last year ... He slipped out of his box and spent the year on the closet floor—

THE NARRATOR (*with a sly smile*)

You could've crushed him during one of the thunderstorms!

His mother shoots him a dirty look. THE NARRATOR leaves the table and wanders off.

Music.

GABRIEL enters and sits down in his mother's rocking chair. He starts listening to a comedy program on an American radio station. He laughs along with the studio audience. The radio cabinet is enormous and GABRIEL is looking at it as if he could see what was happening at the other end of the American continent. ALBERTINE is sitting at the dining room table, hemming the sleeve of a powder blue satin dress with a tulle overskirt. THE NARRATOR enters and sits down in his armchair.

ALBERTINE

Gabriel ... It's five to nine on Thursday night ... *Ford Theatre* starts in five minutes ...

GABRIEL

Oh, Christ ... you're not going to make us listen to that crap again ...

ALBERTINE

Hey! Tonight it's Germaine Giroux in *La danseuse rouge.* They say she plays a Russian spy who's mean as anything and she tortures poor Marjolaine Hébert who makes you so sad you could cry. I wouldn't miss it for anything in the world ... So just too bad, go to bed if you're not interested!

GABRIEL

It's only nine o'clock! I usually work 'til midnight and I never go to bed before two in the morning!

She glances at him.

ALBERTINE

Still haven't found anything?

GABRIEL

They said they'd probably call me back in the New Year ...

ALBERTINE

Go work somewhere else.

GABRIEL

It's worse in other places.

ALBERTINE

When Nana saw you come home with your toolbox a couple of weeks ago, I thought she was going to faint ... Make an effort, look around a bit ...

GABRIEL

Hey, you might be my sister, but that doesn't give you the right to judge me.

ALBERTINE

I'm not judging you ...

GABRIEL

Yes, you are! You seem to think I like being unemployed.

ALBERTINE

I never said that.

GABRIEL

Maybe, but you're so obvious, sometimes I can hear you thinking!

ALBERTINE

Well, all you do is sit around day after day and wait for the shop to call you back. They're not the only printers in town!

GABRIEL

But I like working there, and they're the ones who give me work.

ALBERTINE

Okay! Fine. Just sit there and listen to Bob Hope and wait. What else can I say?

After a brief silence, he turns the radio down, gets up and walks over to the table. He points to the dress.

GABRIEL

Almost finished?

ALBERTINE

I can't believe I'm doing this ...

GABRIEL (*laughing*)

I can hardly wait.

ALBERTINE

Well, not me ... It's Édouard's job to play the clown in the family, not mine!

GABRIEL

He's not free this year ...

ALBERTINE

He's not free this year, my eye! He could've arrived at that party for his friend Samarcette a bit late, that's all. What's the problem—

GABRIEL

It's a supper party, Bartine!

ALBERTINE

He could've arrived for dessert! He could've jumped out of the cake in his Santa costume. He wouldn't even have needed to change to make his buddies laugh! He's never around to help us out, that's for sure ...

GABRIEL

That's not true, Bartine, this is the first time it's happened.

ALBERTINE

After the first time, there's always a second ... And believe me, there's no way I'm going to do this every year!

GABRIEL

Fine, but you're wasting your breath now. You got the job this year, period!

ALBERTINE

Yeah, great! What am I supposed to say to him? How am I supposed to talk? That kid's too smart not to recognize me!

GABRIEL

He doesn't recognize Édouard when he sees him in his Santa costume ...

ALBERTINE

That's what you think! I'm sure he recognized him the first time he saw him, when he was only six months old!

GABRIEL

Then he'll act the same way with you.

ALBERTINE

I bet he'll laugh in my face and I'll let him get away with it!

THE NARRATOR has stood up and come closer to them.
ALBERTINE is startled and tries in vain to hide the dress that is much too voluminous.

ALBERTINE

My God, you scared me! Where did you come from? I thought you went to your aunt Béa's with your mother to listen to *La danseuse rouge?*

THE NARRATOR

No ... I had a stomach ache and I went to bed ... Mama told you but you never listen ... I've come to listen to *Ford Theatre* with you. What are you doing?

ALBERTINE

Well ... uh ...

She looks to GABRIEL who shrugs helplessly.

ALBERTINE

Nothing special ... just mending ... an old dress ...

THE NARRATOR

An old dress made out of new satin?

GABRIEL smiles and slips away on his tiptoes.

ALBERTINE

(*to GABRIEL*) Coward! (*to her nephew*) Well ... I don't know what to tell you ... I should come up with something, but I can't ... You always have to know everything, it's a real pain ... (*She explodes.*) You want to know what I'm doing? Is that it? Well, let me tell you! I'm preparing to make a fool of myself, that's what I'm doing! Is that clear? Nothing complicated about it ... in a few days, I'm gonna make a fool of myself, so everyone can laugh at me like I've never been laughed at before! And people will talk about it for years! When you go to university twenty years from now, you'll tell your friends about it and they'll never believe that one of your aunts made such a fool of herself. I'm preparing to do something that somebody else usually does, but that somebody else has something better to do that night, instead of doing what he usually does! It's that simple! I've been elected to do it, I don't feel like it, I don't want to do it, but I'm stuck doing it even if I know that it's hopeless because I'm no good at this kind of thing. I'll probably freeze and on top of making a fool of myself, I'll make everyone feel so embarrassed, it'll be awful! That's what I'm doing! And you know what? You just made me miss the beginning of *La danseuse rouge,* and I won't watch the rest because I hate missing the beginning of things, I'd rather miss the whole damn thing than miss part of it! Just because of you, I'll never know what Germaine Giroux does to make Marjolaine Hébert suffer, until your mother tells me about it, clutching her heart with both hands because it was so beautiful, and that will piss me off even more! Good night!

> *She exits, dragging her powder blue dress behind her.*
>
> *The lighting changes.*
>
> *VICTOIRE enters with some strings of Christmas tree lights she has just untangled. She is wearing them the way one would wear leis of flowers. She looks decorated herself. NANA enters behind her.*

VICTOIRE

Took me almost two hours to untangle these ... It happens every year. No matter how often I tell them to put them away carefully, they always stuff the darn lights into their boxes any ole way. They get all tangled up, you have to push and pull ... I'm telling you, Nana, we almost ended up with no lights on the tree this year. I almost threw the whole mess out my bedroom window!

NANA

You say that every year, Madame Tremblay.

VICTOIRE

If Gabriel and the kids listened to me for once, I wouldn't have to repeat myself all the time ... And I wouldn't have to fight with this every December!

NANA

And you'd be bored stiff.

VICTOIRE

What's that supposed to mean?

NANA

Nothing. Never mind. I've almost finished putting the hooks on the ornaments.

VICTOIRE

I'd like to know why you do that every year ... If you left the hooks on them when we take down the tree, you wouldn't have to start over again every year ...

NANA gives her mother-in-law a look. VICTOIRE shrugs.

VICTOIRE

Fine. I didn't say a thing. Do as you please ... We can go on buying a package of new hooks every year because the old ones are all scrambled up in a rat's nest and have to be thrown out. There's a lot of waste goes on in this house.

NANA

Especially a lot of wasted saliva.

VICTOIRE

Whoa, let's drop the comments for tonight. You're pretty crabby all of a sudden.

NANA

I just had another useless discussion with my kid.

VICTOIRE

Well, that's better than having a useless discussion with an adult!

NANA

Looks like Christmas is going to be a barrel of fun this year! (*Beat.*) And as far as the hooks go, I'll have you know I enjoy doing that! Putting them on the ornaments makes me feel like I'm preparing for an important event ... I take the ornaments out and wipe them off ... one by one ... I know them all! I could tell you where every single one of them comes from! Next thing you know I'll be giving them all names. And when I take them off the tree two weeks later, it means that important event is over ... and I get to look at them again, before putting them away till the following year. I take off the hooks and put them back in their box, one by one ...

VICTOIRE

Well, if you don't mind wasting your time like that—

NANA

It's not a waste of time ... And if it is, what difference does it make to you? You won't get your snack any later tonight just because I put the hooks on the Christmas tree ornaments. So don't complain!

VICTOIRE

No need to get mad, Nana, we're just chatting ... Speaking of eating, that reminds me ... I hope ... I hope you didn't buy synonym again for the apple pies ...

NANA

I know you don't like cinnamon, Madame Tremblay—

VICTOIRE

I know your side of the family likes it ... if she could, your mother would dab it on under her arms as perfume ...

NANA

I told you, I get the picture, Madame Tremblay ... what more do you want?

VICTOIRE

Well, I just want to be sure! Synonym's an English Canadian thing ... something they got from the States, probably. They put the stuff in everything! It's like they came into this world sucking on a synonym pacifier! On my side of the family, we hate it so much, we don't even put it in our synonym-buns!

NANA

They say it's good for us—

VICTOIRE

That's not true! You'd make up anything, just to get your way!

NANA

Well, a lot of poor people would be happy to have some.

VICTOIRE

I'm poor and I'm not happy to have some! I should've thrown the tin out last year, I knew it ...

NANA

Don't you let me catch you throwing out my cinnamon!

VICTOIRE

It smells too strong. It's too overwhelming, that's all there is
to it! You just have to cook one pie with synonym in it and
you feel like it's in all the pies! The chicken we cook in the
oven afterwards smells of synonym. The tea smells of
synonym! The dishwater smells of synonym. The toilet
smells of synonym! The garbage smells of synonym!

NANA

My God, you've got a real grudge against cinnamon today!

VICTOIRE

I'm afraid it's going to show up in my apple pie! I like apple
pie too much to spoil it with that stuff! I'm going to kill
someone if I find any in my apple pie—is that clear?

NANA

And I wonder who that someone will be? Eh?

VICTOIRE

I'm not going to let you win, Nana! Otherwise the ice box
will smell of synonym for weeks! Our hair will smell of
synonym, our clothes will smell of synonym, the 'ninoleum
in the kitchen will smell of synonym …

> ALBERTINE *arrives in the meantime, carrying a huge box.*

ALBERTINE

I finally found the goddamn box of garlands! (*NANA and
VICTOIRE point to beneath the table, although THE NARRATOR has
not returned there.*) What?! Just because I said goddamn?
C'mon, he hears a lot worse when his father's three sheets
to the wind. (*She places the box on the floor.*) I'd forgotten
where I put it away.

VICTOIRE

It's hard to miss …

ALBERTINE

I put it upright at the back of the closet, behind the old
rolled-up rug … I looked in there twenty-five times before I
saw it … (*She has opened the box.*) I say it every year, and I'm
saying it again—these garlands are so old and dirty and ugly,
I'd like to throw them in the trash can. It looks like we fried
a hundred steaks right under them! They're as greasy as the
kitchen ceiling over the stove.

NANA

Give me a budget to buy some new ones, and you'll never have to look at them again!

ALBERTINE (*with a sly smile*)

Well, I guess they're not so bad. They should last us another twenty years! (*NANA and VICTOIRE laugh. ALBERTINE takes out a garland and holds it up to the tree.*) Can't you just see them in twenty years? The tree will be draped in brown turds! (*She looks toward the table.*) Maybe by then he won't be under the table anymore ... (*NANA slaps her on the hand. The three women laugh.*) I can see him at twenty-five, squatting under the table, eavesdropping on us ... Then we'll really have to make sure we keep our knees together ...

NANA

So here we are, ready to start, and his lordship's nowhere in sight.

We hear GABRIEL doing voice warm-up exercises offstage.

ALBERTINE

Speaking of the devil, it won't be long ...

NANA

Don't tell me we're going to get another performance of "Ninety-nine bottles of beer"!

VICTOIRE

You know what that means.

NANA

Oh, yes. The Normand Tavern ... Home of the unemployed ...

The three women raise their eyes to heaven. GABRIEL enters, wearing his hat.

GABRIEL (*repeating the words to the song as he heard them*)*
Ninety-nine bottles of beer on the wall
Ninety-nine bottles of cheer
If one of those bottles happens to call
There'll be ninety-eight bottles left for us all ...

---

* In the original French script, Gabriel, who is hard of hearing, sings "Le petit vin blanc," rendering the lyrics as he hears them. As an English equivalent, I have substituted the popular "99 bottles of beer," with approximate lyrics. [L.G.]

NANA

Your hat, Gabriel!

GABRIEL

What about it?

NANA

It's still on your head!

GABRIEL takes it off, laughing.

GABRIEL

We should hang it at the top of the tree, instead of your damn cardboard angel ... It might look real pretty with a light inside.

ALBERTINE

At least it wouldn't be as ugly as that ugly angel!

NANA

Bartine! Don't start in on my angel again!

ALBERTINE

An angel at the top of the tree, instead of a beautiful star, is ugly! When are you going to understand that?

GABRIEL (*staggering just a bit*)

It's true it's not very pretty ...

NANA

Are you going to be able to climb that ladder?

GABRIEL (*hand on his heart*)

For you, I'd climb Mount Everest barefoot!

NANA (*holding her angel like a precious object*)

Of course, we all know that ... but that's not what I'm asking ...

GABRIEL

Give it to me, it'll be up there in less than a minute. It'll be ugly as sin, but it'll be there!

NANA

Yeah, and maybe there'll be nothing left of the tree, or the angel!

GABRIEL

Oh ye of little faith!

NANA

It's just the voice of experience speaking. Go on, climb the ladder, you're the only one around here who's not afraid of heights ... when you haven't had too much to drink!

GABRIEL sets the stepladder up beside the tree.

NANA

I don't understand you people ... this angel is so beautiful ...

ALBERTINE

It's not the angel itself that's ugly, it's pretty enough, it's just that—

She looks at her mother, hoping she'll come to her rescue.

VICTOIRE

It's just that ... Well ... that's not what goes at the top of a Christmas tree, Nana!

ALBERTINE

There should be a star!!

VICTOIRE

A star is what goes at the top of a Christmas tree!

GABRIEL

Okay, pass the thing to me ...

NANA

I know that! But aren't you glad that your Christmas tree is different from everyone else's on the street?!

ALBERTINE and VICTOIRE look at each other.

GABRIEL

Nana ...

VICTOIRE AND ALBERTINE

No.

GABRIEL

Pass me the angel, Nana ...

VICTOIRE

We don't want it to be different ...

ALBERTINE

We want it to be the same ... just more beautiful! More beautiful is fine, but ... different—

GABRIEL

Nana, have you gone deaf all of a sudden?

NANA

You know what I feel like doing with this angel right now? If the kid wasn't hiding under the table, if he couldn't hear me, I'd tell you what I'd do with this angel, and I'd have to go to confession afterwards! First the cinnamon, now the angel … Is there anything I do right in this house? Am I ruining your lives?

VICTOIRE

Good Lord, Nana!

ALBERTINE

C'mon …

GABRIEL

Don't get mad like that, you're white as a sheet.

VICTOIRE

It's just that whenever anyone comes into this house at Christmas time, the first thing they say is: "Look at that … you've got an angel at the top of your tree … That's weird, isn't it supposed to be a star?"

NANA passes the angel to her husband.

NANA

Well, they're ignorant people, with no imagination … If it's so important to you, we'll discuss it again next year … *Before* we put up the tree! You can go buy a big, ugly star, so we can copy other people, like dumb sheep, and our tree will be the same as everyone else's!

GABRIEL (*to charm her*)

Is it the Archangel Gabriel?

NANA

Hell will freeze over before I put your portrait at the top of my Christmas tree …

As he installs the angel, NANA hands him a string of lights.

NANA

If you string the lights at the top of the tree, we can do the ones farther down …

GABRIEL

I don't mind doing them all, you know …

NANA

The state you're in, I'm not sure how long I can trust you up there …

GABRIEL leans over towards her.

GABRIEL (*quietly*)

I just had a couple of beers, Nana ... I'm fine ... In control ... Don't worry ...

He staggers a bit and grabs onto a branch.

GABRIEL

That's just because I was leaning over ...

He starts to string the lights on the branches, humming to regain his composure. NANA turns to ALBERTINE.

NANA

Don't you have something else to do?

ALBERTINE

Me? No ...

NANA

Bartine ...

NANA points to beneath the dining table.

ALBERTINE

What?

VICTOIRE

Bartine! Do we have to draw you a picture? Don't you have something to do when your uncle Josaphat gets here, any minute now?!

THE NARRATOR

Uncle Josaphat's on his way? Yippee!

ALBERTINE reacts.

ALBERTINE

Oh, right! It's true! My God! I forgot about that! Dammit ...

She exits almost running.

NANA

By the time I go to bed tonight, I'll be so exhausted, I'll sleep until Epiphany!

GABRIEL

Pass me the other lights ... Hey, by the way, did you make sure they're working?

The two women look at each other.

VICTOIRE

Uhhhhh ... .

NANA (*innocently*)

Do you remember if they were all working last year, Gabriel?

GABRIEL

Oh, shit!

> *NANA doesn't have time to react, before JOSAPHAT enters with his raccoon coat over his shoulders. His entrance is more successful than GABRIEL's, since GABRIEL in fact was trying to imitate him.*

JOSAPHAT (*to the tune of "April in Paris"*)*

> *April's in Paris,*
> *Her chest is in blossom*
> *Holding her suitors down on their knees*
> *April's in Paris, my heart is reeling*
> *Just let me grab what I please ...*

> *ALBERTINE has come back in time to hear the end of the song.*

VICTOIRE

Josaphat! Mind the child!

JOSAPHAT

Well, well, well, look who's here! My favourite kid sister!

ALBERTINE (*through gritted teeth*)

Oh yes ... we all know that ...

> *She glances at her brother, still perched at the top of the stepladder.*

VICTOIRE

Don't come near me, I don't want to smell your beer breath ...

JOSAPHAT

Just a teeny-weeny kiss ... (*VICTOIRE struggles. JOSAPHAT gives up.*) So, Nana, how 'bout you, or my sweet, gentle Albertine? ...

ALBERTINE

If you come near me, I'll strangle you with a greasy garland!

> *She exits.*

---

* In the original French, Josaphat enters singing his bawdy lyrics to the tune of "Douce France." As an English equivalent, I have suggested "April in Paris," a classic from the '30s, popular throughout the '40s and '50s. [L.G.]

THE NARRATOR (*to lighten the mood*)

How are you, Uncle Josaphat?

JOSAPHAT

If I felt any better, boy, it would mean that I was in Heaven, sitting at the right hand of God, on Saint Geneviève de Brabant's lap, and she'd be wearing next to nothing ... And believe me, she wouldn't be playing with her harp!

VICTOIRE

How can a man say things like that in front of a child his age!

JOSAPHAT

He doesn't understand.

VICTOIRE

A good thing, too! You don't smell of beer tonight, you smell of hard liquor ...

JOSAPHAT

Christmas only comes once a year ...

VICTOIRE

I hope you don't have a fifth hidden in the pocket of your raccoon coat, like last year ...

JOSAPHAT (*as he takes off his raccoon coat*)

You can search me ... I took care of business before coming here because I knew it would be a dry evening ... Candy is dandy but liquor is quicker.

VICTOIRE

You didn't come here to drink ... I hope you're sober enough to do your job right, for once!

JOSAPHAT (*almost whispering*)

Don't worry, I arranged everything with Édouard ... He's expecting my phone call ...

VICTOIRE (*sternly, again*)

I hope you haven't prepared one of your dumb jokes again ... (*passing him a dish of candies*) Here, try one, it might improve your breath ... I don't want you breathing your booze breath into that child's face ...

JOSAPHAT

Great! Goldfish! My favourites!

VICTOIRE (*smiling in spite of herself*)
    A real kid …

THE NARRATOR
    Can I have one, too?

VICTOIRE
    Here, sweetheart, but don't eat too many, they'll make you
    sick …

    THE NARRATOR helps himself. So does VICTOIRE.

VICTOIRE
    Mmmm. It's true, these are good.

NANA (*as she helps her husband with the strings of lights*)
    I'd like to point out, Madame Tremblay, that goldfish are
    made with *synonym.*

    VICTOIRE looks shocked and spits out the candy.

JOSAPHAT (*to the Narrator*)
    Now that I've got no breath, I can say hello to you … come
    give your uncle Josaphat a kiss.

    THE NARRATOR goes over to him and they hug.

THE NARRATOR
    Santa Claus didn't come with you this year? He usually
    comes to help us decorate the Christmas tree …

NANA (*bitterly*)
    No, he was too busy this year …

VICTOIRE
    Nana …

NANA
    He's never let me down like this before …

VICTOIRE
    It'll all work out. Bartine had time to whip something up.

NANA
    That's what I'm worried about …

THE NARRATOR (*to his uncle*)
    Have you known him for a long time?

JOSAPHAT (*who was listening to the two women*)
    Who? Your uncle Édouard?

THE NARRATOR
    No! Santa Claus!

JOSAPHAT

Ah, that old rascal! Of course I've known him for a long time. (*quietly, aside to his sister*)

Isn't he getting a bit old for this stuff?

VICTOIRE

That's what I've been trying to tell Nana for ages ...

NANA

I want him to remain a child for as long as he wants ...

JOSAPHAT

I hope he won't show up like that on his wedding night ...

Both men laugh.

VICTOIRE

Josaphat!

JOSAPHAT (*to THE NARRATOR*)

But I've already told you that story a hundred times.

THE NARRATOR

I don't care ... Tell me again ...

JOSAPHAT

Why not ... today it'll be different anyway, 'cause the show's going to have a different ending—

NANA

Watch what you say, uncle ...

GABRIEL

You can lay it on, gild the lily as much as you want, he'll love it ... Stories are never long enough for him ...

NANA

We all know the kind of stories you like!

GABRIEL

Yes, short and spicy, and I can hardly wait to tell him a few!

She slaps his hand.

NANA

I'll let you know when the time comes ...

GABRIEL

I've got the feeling it's going to be a while! If he shows up on his wedding night still believing in Santa Claus, he won't understand my stories.

The men laugh.

JOSAPHAT

> You better believe it. He'll be pretty surprised by the Santa that pops out of his pants.

VICTOIRE

> Now don't start that, the two of you ...

JOSAPHAT (*taking her by the waist*)

> Okay, okay ... beginning right now, I'll give him the expurgated version of his uncle Josaphat ...

GABRIEL

> My God, what's with the two-foot long words, Uncle?

JOSAPHAT

> Just because a guy's vulgar once in a while, doesn't mean he's got no vocabulary, boy.

VICTOIRE

> Once in a while?

JOSAPHAT (*slapping her on the bum*)

> You can't kid me ... you act holier-than-thou, but you love it when I tease you. And you get a kick out my dirty jokes, don't you?

> > *He bows low in front of her. During the following scene, the other two adults will act as if they don't notice a thing and continue to decorate the tree.*

VICTOIRE

> Josaphat, have another candy! I can smell liquor again!

JOSAPHAT (*with a sly look*)

> Are you still a widow, Mademoiselle?

VICTOIRE

> Where's a woman my age who spends her days locked up here going to meet someone? Besides, I'm not interested, not at all and you know it, don't make me waste my breath.

JOSAPHAT

> But you're still as enticing as ever ...

> > *She stares at him before answering.*

VICTOIRE

> Me, enticing? Now I've heard everything ...

JOSAPHAT

> Do you still have that beauty mark behind your left knee?

VICTOIRE

What I've got these days behind my left knee hasn't been a beauty mark for years. There's nothing beautiful about it.

JOSAPHAT

Well, it would be beautiful to me!

VICTOIRE smoothes her dress on her knees.

VICTOIRE

Don't start in on that, Josaphat. When you've been drinking, you say things we have to pretend we didn't hear ... things that are hard *for me* to forget afterwards ... And some things are better forgotten. Let sleeping dogs lie.

JOSAPHAT (*suddenly serious*)

But I don't want you to forget them. I want you to wake those dogs up. It might do you good.

VICTOIRE (*for a change of mood*)

The closer you come, the more I think you need more goldfish, Josaphat.

JOSAPHAT dips into the dish of goldfish and turns to THE NARRATOR with a neat pirouette.

JOSAPHAT

On your mark, get set, go! (*to THE NARRATOR*) Actually, Santa Claus and I are about the same age ...

THE NARRATOR

What? Santa's that old?

JOSAPHAT

No, I guess I'm a bit older than him. He was a year behind me at grade school, or maybe two, something like that—

THE NARRATOR

You went to school together!

JOSAPHAT

Yep, and I was a better student than him! He wasn't too bright, Santa ... All he knew how to do was his ho-ho-ho's and his ha-ha-ha's—

VICTOIRE (*cutting him off*)

Josaphat ...

JOSAPHAT (*resuming his story*)

 It's not that he wasn't too bright, he was just ... a real daydreamer. He always said that one day he'd spend Christmas Eve travelling around ...

THE NARRATOR

 Really?

JOSAPHAT

 None of us believed him, of course ... And he looked silly in his little red outfit with the white angora fluff around the cuffs ...

VICTOIRE

 Josaphat ...

THE NARRATOR

 He already dressed in red when he was in school!

JOSAPHAT (*to his sister*)

 C'mon, if you keep interrupting me after every two words ...

VICTOIRE (*raising her voice a bit*)

 It's not my fault, Josaphat. You say something stupid every two words.

JOSAPHAT (*same tone*)

 It's a story, Victoire, and Gabriel just told me to gild the lily!

THE NARRATOR

 Stop fighting, the two of you. I don't like that.

VICTOIRE

 We're not fighting ...

JOSAPHAT

 We're having a loud discussion ...

THE NARRATOR

 Then I don't like your loud discussions ...

GABRIEL

 Well, you landed in the wrong family, boy ...

NANA

 Gabriel, stay out of it.

THE NARRATOR

 Don't you start fighting now, too.

JOSAPHAT (*with a conciliatory gesture*)

 Okay, okay ... Why don't the three of you concentrate on that superb Christmas tree you're decorating, and let me concentrate on my story—okay? Is it a deal? Otherwise, we'll still be here on New Year's Eve and my buddy Santa won't have had time to grow up and become Santa Claus.

The others turn away and concentrate on the tree.

JOSAPHAT

I know you're going to listen, but I'd appreciate it if you stopped interrupting me! So, now! (*to THE NARRATOR*) What did you ask me?

THE NARRATOR

You say he went to school dressed in red ... with white angora on his sleeves ... I don't believe the angora part, but that's all right, I think it's funny ...

JOSAPHAT

You mean you don't believe everything I say?

THE NARRATOR

I'm used to Mama's stories, Uncle ...

His mother looks at him, but doesn't dare speak. THE NARRATOR smiles.

THE NARRATOR

Has it been a long time since you saw him?

JOSAPHAT

Well, I can't say that we hang out together regularly, but he was here with me last year when we decorated the tree, remember?

THE NARRATOR

I don't mean that Santa, I mean the real one who went to school with you ...

JOSAPHAT glances at the other adults before continuing.

JOSAPHAT (*a bit lost*)

Well, uhhh ... You better believe it's been a long time since I saw him ... He was just beginning his career as a distributor of toys back then! But I've still got his telephone number. Unless he's changed it ...

THE NARRATOR

You've got Santa's telephone number?!

JOSAPHAT

Hold on. I'm sure I've got it somewhere ... (*He takes out his wallet.*) Wait, I had a little notebook. It was black ... Ah, there it is … (*He thumbs through his notebook.*) So … hmmm … Cinderella … Pinocchio … It's farther on … Snow White … Oops, I've gone too far … Ah ha, there we go: Santa Claus!

THE NARRATOR

You have all those numbers!

JOSAPHAT

And those are just the numbers I dare mention. You should see my shocking pink notebook.

VICTOIRE

Josaphat!

JOSAPHAT

Mae West, Paula Negri, Mata-Hari …

VICTOIRE

Josaphat! He doesn't even know who those women are! You're just trying to get a rise out of me!

THE NARRATOR

Who are those women, Uncle Josaphat?

JOSAPHAT

My old girl friends … Your grandmother doesn't approve of them …

THE NARRATOR

Why not?

JOSAPHAT (*looking at his sister*)

I guess you'll have to ask her some day …

THE NARRATOR

Are they … (*lowering his voice, almost whispering*) floozies?

NANA

Where did you get that?

THE NARRATOR

When the three of you talk about them, you always lower your voices …

NANA

I don't believe we ever talked about that in front of you!

THE NARRATOR

Sometimes you forget that I'm there …

VICTOIRE (*to NANA*)

You see, for once Bartine's the one who's right. You didn't give birth to a child, you gave birth to one big ear.

GABRIEL

And a stomach, too, because I'm telling you, that kid packs it in! On top of everything else, he'll probably be too fat on his wedding night!

JOSAPHAT

Hey, can I get on with my show, if you don't mind?

NANA

Go ahead … (*to her son*) But we have to have a talk …

THE NARRATOR (*to change the subject*)

I want to talk to him!

JOSAPHAT (*hypocritically*)

Talk to who?

THE NARRATOR

To Santa! Who do you think? Is it the same as the number for heaven? I called that number once, but there was no answer … It was my brother Coco who gave it to me, but you know how he mixes up his telephone numbers …

VICTOIRE

That's not the only thing he mixes up, poor guy …

NANA

Here we go again!

JOSAPHAT

Well, it's not the same number. To call Heaven you have to go through the Bell operator, but to speak to Santa Claus, you can dial direct. Because the number I've got is his personal number …

THE NARRATOR

You have Santa Claus's personal number?!

JOSAPHAT

I'll dial it for you … Come stand on my knees or your mouth won't reach the horn and Santa won't be able to hear you … He'll think it's someone playing a joke and he'll hang up … Now watch where you put your feet! Last time, your uncle had tears in his eyes for hours because you went stomping around in a pretty sensitive region … and your uncle had a squeaky little voice for days …

> THE NARRATOR *can hardly contain himself as* JOSAPHAT *dials the number.* NANA *looks concerned.*

NANA

> I think that's enough of your crazy stories, Uncle Josaphat. You're going to make the child sick—

THE NARRATOR

> What crazy stories? It's not a crazy story! Is it, Uncle? Tell her it's not a crazy story!

JOSAPHAT

> Shhh ... it's ringing!

> > *NANA rolls her eyes.*

JOSAPHAT

> I'd like to speak to Mr. Claus, please. (*He puts his hand over the receiver.*) I think it was one of his elves.

THE NARRATOR (*excited*)

> It's the right place! It's the right number!

JOSAPHAT

> He went to get Santa ... (*looking at the others*) I'm telling you, it sounds pretty busy there ... You should hear the racket at the other end of the line, it's pretty wild ...

NANA (*smiling in spite of herself*)

> I wonder if Samarcette was really surprised ...

JOSAPHAT

> Hello? What? His brother! (*to THE NARRATOR*) We don't want to speak to Santa's brother, do we?

> > *THE NARRATOR stares at him incredulously.*

THE NARRATOR

> Santa Claus has a brother?!

JOSAPHAT (*shouting into the receiver*)

> I want to speak to Santa Claus! That's right, Santa, himself, in person, and nobody else! (*He leans over to his nephew.*) He's coming. I think he went to the john ...

> > *VICTOIRE lets out an exasperated sigh. GABRIEL bursts out laughing.*

JOSAPHAT

> And when he goes to the john, it's his brother Clovis who takes the orders for him. But he doesn't know his ass from his elbow and he'll tell you any ole thing ... You can't believe a word Clovis Claus tells you. You have to make sure you talk to Mr. Santa Claus himself! Hello, Santa? How's it

84

going, you ole sonofagun? Still dragging your sack around town? Don't you recognize me? It's Josaphat. Josaphat-the-fiddle ... Formerly of Duhamel, currently residing in the East End. Damn right, I'm still a fiddler! You know what they say: Once a fiddler, always a fiddler. How 'bout you? Still so fat? And your wife's raisin pies still as good as ever? Her mince meat pies still so greasy? Last time I had one I was burping for months! My chocolate Easter bunny tasted of mince meat! (*Pause.*) On a diet! Oh, her, not you! Good thing! A skinny Santa Claus, be worse than Baby Jesus without a halo! Or the Virgin Mary dressed in canary yellow! Scare the kids to death! Hey, listen, I can't talk too long, it's long distance, you know, it costs an arm and a leg and my nephew Gabriel's a real cheapskate, but there's somebody here beside me who'd like to have a few words with you ... His name is Michel, he wasn't really a good boy this year, but we let him get away with it, if you know what I mean ... Right ... Spoiled rotten ... Right ... A real pain sometimes ... What do you expect, his parents let him get away with murder ... So does his grandmother ... And his godmother too ... Okay, bye, now, don't forget to say hello to Claudia for me. If I trusted the mail, I'd tell her to send me a couple of her raisin pies, but they'd probably arrive like soup! And I never been able to digest pie soup ...

    GABRIEL bursts out laughing again.

GABRIEL
    Honestly, Uncle Josaphat, Claudia!

JOSAPHAT (*proud of his joke*)
    What's the matter? You don't think Claudia Claus is a good name for his wife?

THE NARRATOR
    I don't want to talk to him now. I'm too shy.

JOSAPHAT
    Michel, it's long distance, c'mon! A direct line to Candyville, the capital of the North Pole! You want us to spend all this money for nothing?

    THE NARRATOR takes the receiver and brings it to his mouth.

THE NARRATOR (*shyly*)
    Hello?

We hear a lot of ho-ho-ho's and and ha-ha-ha's. THE
NARRATOR relaxes and smiles.

THE NARRATOR

Are you busy preparing our Christmas toys, Santa? 'Cause
there's only three days left.

Santa Claus laughs a lot, maybe a bit too much, because THE
NARRATOR frowns a bit.

THE NARRATOR

You're not drinking beer, are you? You're laughing like my
uncles when they've had too much to drink!

More laughter.

THE NARRATOR

What's that noise in the background? (*He listens.*) They've
got really loud voices for elves! What? They're finishing the
toys! What am I getting this year? What are my toys? Tell me!
(*He listens and frowns again. Then, to JOSAPHAT:*) Santa just
said "for Cripe's sake," just like uncle Édouard!

VICTOIRE (*trying to cover up for her son*)

Tell him it's not nice to say that ...

NANA

And this is no time to say it!

THE NARRATOR

My grandmother says ... Oh, you heard her ... So, don't say
it again! (*resuming his train of thought*) Is my electric train a
Lionel, like I asked for? Oh, you're right, it's supposed to be
a surprise ... Well, I'll act surprised, I promise ... What? Yes,
I know, long distance is expensive ... Well ... are you going
to eat my mother's apple pie, like last year? (*He listens, then,*
to his mother:) Santa wants to know if you're going to put
cinnamon in it ... (*He listens.*) If you are, he'd rather have
doughnuts!

VICTOIRE makes a victory sign.

JOSAPHAT

Okay, now, blow Santa some nice kisses ... we don't want to
keep him too long ...

THE NARRATOR

Bye, bye, Santa Claus! (*He listens briefly.*) What? What
assistant? Really! The Christmas Fairy's coming here!

When? No, she hasn't arrived yet! … Okay, I'll wait for her.
Bye!

> *THE NARRATOR blows two or three kisses into the receiver and
> hangs up.*

THE NARRATOR
I spoke to Santa Claus, Mama!

NANA (*between gritted teeth*)
Yeah, the big party boy who says "for Cripe's sake" every
other word.

THE NARRATOR
And he says that the Christmas Fairy will be here any minute
now. I guess she's replacing him this year, to help decorate
the trees.

NANA
I hope you're going to give her a good welcome.

THE NARRATOR
Of course, I will. The Christmas Fairy—that's amazing!

> *The doorbell rings.*

VICTOIRE
That must be her!

THE NARRATOR
The Christmas Fairy's here. The Christmas Fairy!

> *He exits, running to answer the door.*

NANA
I hope this works out.

GABRIEL
Dream on.

JOSAPHAT
Poor Bartine, she's got as much imagination as a doorpost.

NANA
How encouraging can you get!

ALBERTINE (*offstage*)
Well, well, well, well, look at that, what an adorrrrrrrrable
little boooy!

VICTOIRE
Oh dear, not a very promising start.

ALBERTINE

What's your name? Eh? Speak up, Auntie … uhhh … the
Fairy can't hear you. Don't tell me you're shy with the
Christmas Fairy!

*ALBERTINE and THE NARRATOR reenter. Albertine is dressed
up like the poor man's version of the Christmas Fairy. She's
wearing the powder blue dress she was sewing at the beginning
of the play and carrying a magic wand she improvised out of a
broomstick or the likes. The tiara on her head is unspeakably
ugly. And to top it all off, she is wearing her own winter coat.
THE NARRATOR isn't fooled and simply stares at her, not
knowing how to react.*

THE NARRATOR (*to his mother*)

That's supposed to be the Christmas Fairy? (*whispering*) My
aunt Bartine?

NANA

Be a good boy and pretend you don't recognize her! I'll
explain everything later …

THE NARRATOR

I'll look stupid!

NANA

Better to look stupid than heartless!

ALBERTINE

Hi, everybody!

ALL TOGETHER

Hello!

ALBERTINE

Santa Claus sends his regards. He's sorry he couldn't come.
It's me, the Christmas Fairy, who's replacing him today …
So, that's it, you're all stuck with me …

She laughs, a phoney laugh.

ALBERTINE

Is that adorrrrable little boy afraid of the Christmas Fairy?
Don't hide behind your mother like that, come see Auntie—

VICTOIRE yanks on her dress.

ALBERTINE

Huh? Oh, right … Come see the good fairy! Aw, now what
did I get myself into? Uhhh … She's travelled a long ways to

come see you, you know, she's no ordinary fairy. She flies
through the air faster than an aeroplane, a real rocket! Just
for you! Just to see you! Just to visit you!

Everyone is horrified by her performance and she realizes it.

ALBERTINE
So ... now ... oh, is that the Christmas tree we have to
decorate? It's a big one, that'll take a while. I'll help you.
The Christmas Fairy is an expert with the tinsel garlands.
Just give her some tinsel garlands and she'll make miracles
with them! (*She is losing face rapidly, but suddenly notices the
angel at the top of the tree.*) Well, look at that, that's funny, it's
not a star at the top of the tree, it's an angel! (*looking at
NANA*) The Christmas Fairy doesn't like angels at the top of
the trees, she prefers stars ... We better change that ... (*to
her nephew*) So, little boy, you better ask your mother to
change that. That's ridiculous, it's ugly, it simply isn't done
... Absolutely have to change that! So, now, let's see ...
should we finish decorating that tree, or do you want to tell
the Christmas Fairy what you want for Christmas right now?
And she'll go tell Santa Claus. Were you a good boy this
year, at least? (*She is clearly exhausted.*) How can I carry on
like this for an hour? I've said everything I've got to say and
I've only been here two minutes! Get me a glass of water, or
something, my mouth is bone dry!

*She laughs, another phoney laugh. Her mother hides her face in
her hands, the two men can't control their laughter.*

THE NARRATOR
Don't bother, Auntie, I recognized you ...

Moment of horrified silence.

ALBERTINE (*still playing her role*)
What's that?

THE NARRATOR
I recognize you, Auntie ...

NANA
Michel, I told you not to do that ...

ALBERTINE
Auntie? Who's Auntie? Where's your Auntie?

89

VICTOIRE
 Bartine, don't bother …
ALBERTINE (*devastated*)
 Okay, but …
THE NARRATOR
 I'm sorry, Auntie …
GABRIEL (*to JOSAPHAT*)
 C'mon, let's go for a smoke in the living room …
VICTOIRE
 Stay right here, you cowards!

 ALBERTINE doesn't budge for a few seconds.

ALBERTINE
 Okay. Fine. I guess … I guess I did all that for nothing! (*She explodes.*) That's right. I did all that for nothing! The dress! The tiara! The magic wand! All that for nothing! I prepared a whole act … I was going to make candies appear with my magic wand and pull a teddy out of a hidden pocket, but I didn't even get that far! I blew it all right away, like an idiot.

 She tosses aside her magic wand, tears off her tiara and takes off her dress.

NANA
 Bartine! Get a hold on yourself!
ALBERTINE
 You and your kid who's too curious for his own good … get him out of my sight before I strangle him!
VICTOIRE
 Bartine, for heaven's sake!
ALBERTINE
 What do you expect, Ma? Do you expect me to take it with a grain of salt? And laugh about it? I can't even make a child of six believe that I'm the Christmas Fairy! He's six years old and he recognized me the minute he opened the door! I saw it in his eyes. I could see the disappointment in his eyes, Ma, and I wished I could die right then and there.
THE NARRATOR
 It's doesn't matter, Auntie …

90

ALBERTINE

Yes, it does matter! (*She's on the verge of tears.*) It really matters! You're too little to understand, but put yourself in my place! I break my back, I kill myself, trying to make you happy, just because fat Édouard is too busy to do his job, then—

VICTOIRE

Bartine ...

ALBERTINE

Oh, we all know, you don't recognize him! You make sure you don't recognize him! Because he's wearing a false beard! I suppose the Christmas Fairy should've worn a false beard so you wouldn't recognize her!

THE NARRATOR

I'm sorry ...

She stares at him briefly.

ALBERTINE

It's all right ... I suppose I'm the one who should apologize—for my lousy performance. Nothing ... Absolutely nothing I do works out! Nothing! Nowhere! Never! No matter how hard I try ...

THE NARRATOR goes over to her and takes her into his arms.

THE NARRATOR

Don't be sad, Auntie ...

ALBERTINE

No matter how hard I try, I do what I can ... but nothing works out, ever!

She is crying.

THE NARRATOR (*to the audience*)

I think we should stop there ... I shouldn't have recognized her ... I should have done her the favour of playing along ... Let's pretend I didn't recognize her ... Fortunately, memory is a mirror we can adjust as we wish. (*ALBERTINE walks away from him.*) Let's take it again from the point where you asked me if I'd been a good boy. (*He turns to her.*) Of course, I was a good boy! Right, Mama, I was good, wasn't I?

NANA (*looking a bit doubtful*)

As good as ... a lump of coal!

GABRIEL
    Come help us ... good fairy ... there's a string of lights that
    doesn't work ... Take out your magic wand ...
JOSAPHAT
    Attaboy ... and think I have a garland you might like ...
VICTOIRE
    Josaphat, your jokes fall so flat I could do my ironing on
    them!
ALBERTINE
    Come here, little boy, the fairy has a great magic trick for
    you ...
        The characters all begin to talk at once.
THE NARRATOR (*to the audience*)
    I'd rather end the evening on a happy note ... All too often,
    the Christmas holidays ended in a crisis ... I'd rather
    remember the happy memories ...
        NANA turns to THE NARRATOR.
NANA
    Haven't you forgotten something?
THE NARRATOR
    What?
        NANA signals for the others to be quiet.
NANA
    You forgot something, or rather ... someone ...
VICTOIRE
    That's right ...
ALBERTINE
    Poor girl ...
THE NARRATOR
    I forgot someone?
GABRIEL
    Of course!
JOSAPHAT
    Lise Allard!
THE NARRATOR
    What!?

VICTOIRE
   Poor girl …
NANA
   We saw her at the very beginning …
ALBERTINE
   She stayed for a couple of minutes …
GABRIEL
   And we never saw her again!
JOSAPHAT
   We don't even know if she's happily married!
GABRIEL
   We'd like to know.
THE NARRATOR
   But I didn't need her, after—
GABRIEL
   So?
NANA
   That's no reason to abandon her like that!
ALBERTINE
   She waited in the wings all that time, twiddling her thumbs!
   She must've been bored stiff!
VICTOIRE
   Look, she's right there …
      They all look in the wings.
JOSAPHAT
   She looks bored to death …
VICTOIRE
   You have us say the stupidest things, when it suits you …
ALBERTINE
   Then you abandon us when you don't need us anymore …
   As if we had nothing to say on our own!
      NANA heads for the wings.
NANA
   Come, Lise, come join us …
      Lise enters, shyly.
NANA
   Let's take a look at you … How's our *lovely nut server?*

LISE ALLARD

Oh, we use it all the time …

VICTOIRE

Don't be shy, come here, so everyone can see you …

LISE stands up straight and waves to the audience, shyly.

JOSAPHAT

Are you happily married?

GABRIEL

Does your husband keep you happy?

NANA

Gabriel! (*pointing to JOSAPHAT*) One is enough, don't you think?

ALBERTINE (*to the NARRATOR*)

Believe me, I'd have a few things to say myself … and I don't need you …

VICTOIRE

Me neither, as far as that goes …

JOSAPHAT

I could write you some plays built on memories, kid … You wouldn't have to make them up!

THE NARRATOR (*smiling*)

Okay, fine … go ahead … have a heyday …

They all begin to tell him stories, including LISE ALLARD. The following monologues will be delivered at the same time, as each character tries to attract THE NARRATOR's attention. THE NARRATOR sits down in the middle of them, beaming happily.

JOSAPHAT

I could tell you my version of the *Chasse-galerie,** the one you love so much, where the Devil himself sails through the sky of the Laurentians in his bark canoe, and Willy Ouellette, the nitwit, swallows his harmonica when the canoe lurches to avoid Piedmont and the Devil has to revive him with shots of Caribou because his magic ointment doesn't work, and

---

* The reference is to the French Canadian legend about *voyageurs* who made a pact with the Devil. In English it is often known as "The Wild Hunt" or "The Bewitched Canoe." In 1991, a 40 cent postage stamp illustrating the legend was issued under the title "Witched Canoe." [L.G.]

me, your uncle Josaphat, Josaphat-the-fiddle in person, arrives to outsmart the Devil in person by replacing his Caribou with holy water ... You must remember that story, it's one of your favourites ... one of the scariest ones ... you never found that story boring!

VICTOIRE

And I could tell you stories, boy, stories that would make your hair stand on end, stories that would make you shake and tremble till the end of your days ... Stories of tragedies too great for the folks they happen to, love stories that make no sense, stories of an impossible love with my own brother and children that are born when they shouldn't be, stories of moves to the city that are useless because they solve nothing at all, entire lives, boy, entire lives spoiled for the love of love, for a forbidden love that refuses to let go, that refuses to die, that refuses to die even though it never should have been born ... Stories that can't be told because the folks they happened to are too ashamed!

NANA

God knows I've told you my share of stories ... Nobody can deny that ... But maybe they weren't the right stories ... Sometimes I wonder and I tell myself that maybe I shouldn't have filled your head with my own questions and doubts, my own problems, that maybe I should've treated you more like a child who's supposed to listen to his mother, and less like someone I enjoyed discussing things with ... Maybe I should've sent you out to play with the other kids when we found you curled up under the table listening to us talk ... Maybe it wasn't ... how should I put it ... maybe it wasn't normal for a little boy to spend his days under a table listening to adults talk! Maybe it wasn't normal! But you loved it so much! And I loved keeping you with me!

ALBERTINE

You know, I always knew that you followed me around for a reason ... That you weren't just listening to me ... you were studying me. Yes, I think that's the right word ... Maybe you didn't realize it yourself, maybe you just found me funny or just plain stupid, but I'd like to believe that you followed me around like that because somehow you found me interesting, too! I'd like to believe that someone, somewhere found me interesting enough to follow me around, to study me ... and to love me. If only you knew how much I would've liked to be the centre of someone's life! I'd like that so much! I can't tell you how much!

GABRIEL

Maybe it's true that I didn't spend enough time with you ... That you were more your mother's son than mine ... And I respected that too much ... Your mother's the one who wanted you so badly, she's the one who wanted another child, and she more or less raised you alone ... And it's true that was partly my fault ... I didn't know my last son as well as I should have ... But that doesn't mean that I didn't care, that I loved you less than the others, it just means what I just said ... You were a present for her, her last chance to have a child, to have the daughter she wanted so badly, and you're the one who showed up, but she loved you like no mother has ever loved a child, and I hope you realize that! I hope you realize that!

LISE ALLARD

What can I tell you? When I got married, I disappeared from your life, we hardly ever saw each other again. And since I know that people's troubles are a lot more interesting to you than their joys, I know that what interests you is why people are unhappy, not why they're happy ... I feel like I should invent some big tragedy, some horrible sickness, even if none of it's true ... But I can't ... I don't feel like it ... I can only tell you that I've been happy ... sure, I've had my share of troubles, like everybody else, the rough patches, the setbacks, but nothing dramatic enough to suit you, nothing that can be exaggerated and turned into a play. I'm sorry to disappoint you ...

They are speaking louder and louder, they are more and more animated, then suddenly ...

BLACKOUT

ALBERTINE (*in the dark*)

Hey! Wait a minute! For once, I've got nothing more to say!

Entrelacs—Montreal, August 2004